Dancing with the Earth Changes

Dancing with the Earth Changes

A Guide through the Challenges of the Twenty-first Century

Marko Pogačnik

UNESCO Artist for Peace

LINDISFARNE BOOKS 2021

Published by Lindisfarne Books
an imprint of SteinerBooks/Anthroposophic Press, Inc.
402 Union Street No. 58, Hudson, New York 12534
www.steinerbooks.org

© Marko Pogačnik 2021

Cover images: Marko Pogačnik
Illustrations: Marko Pogačnik

Flap cosmogram: *Human Being Dancing with Gaia* by Marko Pogačnik

ISBN 978-1-58420-946-1 (paperback)
ISBN 978-1-58420-947-8 (ebook)

Printed in the United States of America

Contents

PART 1: The Known Earth Is Disappearing

1. Unexpected dimensions of the planetary change   10

2. The new Earth exists beyond the exclusive logical explanations   14

3. It is impossible to solve the emerging ecological and social challenges at only the physical level—the archetypal levels call for attention   18

4. The subtle powers of dragons and their life-giving breath   21

5. New conditions for life are coming into existence—No Fear!   27

6. Exercises of perception and communication with the worlds of nature   33

7. The Earth is giving birth to an age of peace and co-existence among all beings   38

PART 2: Personal Aspects of the Planetary Change

1. Gaia offers the possibility of a quantum leap in personal evolution   44

2. The human being as a creature of the Earth—a close relative of the animals   52

3. The elemental self of the human being in relation to our spiritual self   59

4. Cooperation with the inner dragon is inevitable   65

5. Dynamite in our personal luggage—overheated yang and other challenges   69

6. Listen to the voice of your inner self and speak with the voice of your heart   76

7. Exercises to walk the path of life in the attitude of a pilgrimage   82

8. Establishing a non-hierarchical and beyond-institutional link to Divinity   88

PART 3: Transmutation of the Earth and Human Culture

1. Possibilities of a relatively peaceful planetary change   94

2. Advantages of cooperating with parallel evolutions
   — dolphins, Sidhe, and Ents   99

3. The culture of exchange with the plant world — animals retreating   109

4. Gaia Sparks, sub-elemental worlds, and the all-pervading plasma
   of life   114

5. The Universal Goddess in her new role as Indigo Gaia   125

6. Counterforces working secretly to undermine the upcoming age
   of peace   133

7. How to be creative in the conditions of dramatic changes   138

8. Transformation of matter — the world appearing as a hologram   143

9. Plan "A" to avoid cataclysms   150

10. Earth Changes, human destiny, a path for hope!   154

Conclusion

How would the creation of a new Earth sphere affect the future of
humanity?   159

APPENDIX

1. A multidimensional model of reality   166

2. How to use Gaia Touch exercises and rituals   169

3. The feminine chakra system   172

4. How to survive in the conditions of intense Earth Changes   176

List of Gaia Touch exercises and rituals   178

About the author   179

Introduction

It is increasingly evident that the dramatic consequences of the Earth's changing process cannot be avoided, that our civilization today is not willing to implement the necessary measures to stop the deterioration of the natural environment. It is up to open-minded individuals and their networks to engage actively where support for Gaia is lacking.

This book offers alternative insights into the process of the Earth Changes, inspiring a deep listening to Gaia, who is the driving force behind the ongoing planetary transformation. My intention is to offer my worldwide work experience in the fields of geomancy and so-called "Earth healing" to enable a better understanding of the complexity of the Earth Changes. I include stories from several of my dreams connected to the theme of the book that will help to elucidate its pictorial language. I also offer various imaginations as well as Gaia Touch and perception exercises to support your attuning to the changing Earth. These imaginations and exercises will simultaneously support Gaia's efforts in creating optimal conditions for the future evolution of humanity and the elemental and spiritual worlds of the planet.

It is clear to me that the cooperation of human beings with Gaia and her elemental worlds is absolutely necessary for the Earth's transmutation to succeed. We human beings, with our creative imaginations and wide ranging consciousness, are the only ones capable of connecting the earthly and cosmic dimensions in this mutual endeavor of re-creating the Earth as a place of peace and cooperation among all beings and all aspects of life.

Marko Pogačnik, Šempas, December 17, 2020

PART 1

The Known Earth Is Disappearing

1
Unexpected dimensions of the planetary change

A few years ago I had a dream that vividly portrayed the situation pushing our civilization toward the brink of an abyss. As often happens, in my dreams I am with a group of tourists traveling in a bus cruising upon the planet Earth. I see this as a symbol of the masses of people moving upon Gaia's planet, disconnected from her essence.

> *The bus stops in a large parking lot. When leaving the bus, I realize*
> *that even though the parking lot is empty, the driver has parked*
> *the bus too close to the edge of a canyon overlooking a mighty river*
> *far below. I find the driver irresponsible in his parking choice. Even*
> *more surprising, I realize that on top of this ultramodern white bus*
> *is growing an intensely green, thick ivy vine. How can this be?*
> *On returning to the bus we realize that the bus has disappeared.*
> *The driver had parked it too close to the edge of the canyon. We*
> *look down the canyon wall to see the bus upright with water to the*
> *level of its windows in the rushing river. The driver declares that the*
> *bus is engineered for such a situation and runs for help. But mean-*
> *while, we see that the water of the river is rising, lifting the bus and*
> *carrying it away. Now the bus is under water—only the beautiful ivy*
> *on its top is proudly riding upon the waves.*

The dream is clearly urging us human beings to realize that the natural catastrophes and repeated political and economic crises surfacing during the last two decades cannot be solved with the means that caused them. We find ourselves at the threshold of unprecedented historic changes of the Earth, its landscapes, and its beings. We need to realize that the bus of our dreams is no longer following the planned tour route. It is being carried now by the river of life, gliding upon a surprisingly different level of existence, as indicated by the green ivy riding upon the waves.

The explanation I perceived for the surprising situation in which we find ourselves is that recently the planet Earth has begun to move the focus of her evolution from an age dominated by the element Earth toward an age of the element Air. The Earth element is one of extreme materialization of all forms of manifested life: landscapes, stones, rivers, plants, human beings, etc. We all are created with distinct and relatively fixed forms. The element Air, however, represents an age governed by the quality of consciousness, or the quality of all-connectedness, of freedom of expression and multidimensionality. The streams of the Air element are free to move wherever the inner call guides them.

As a result of this transition process, we see on one side the natural environments collapsing, while on the other, it is possible to perceive a new kind of space structure appearing at the subtle levels of existence that can be understood as the future constitution of the planetary environment. The parallel breaking down of social and political security presents a call to change our human attitudes toward nature, the Earth, our fellow beings, and even our own essence.

We are experiencing the natural evolution of the Earth through the four elements. One can imagine the first Earth epoch as the age of the Fire element, the creation of Gaia – the Earth soul – manifested in light particles. The geological interpretation of the Fire epoch is the formation of the molten planet Earth. This epoch was followed by the age of the element of Water, when all aspects of planetary life appeared as information stored in water drops. The Greek philosopher Plato gave it the name "Atlantis." The biblical image of a Great Flood covering all cities and human cultures can be interpreted as planetary life manifested in water crystals. Even now the human body is mainly composed of water.

The present epoch of Gaia's incarnation, our densest form of existence, associated with the process of materialization, is the Earth element. We reside there now, together with plants, animals, and stones, embodied in physical form. The mechanistic culture of the twenty-first century represents its densest possible expression. The continuation of materialization to its conclusion will result in a lifeless planet, with a density too great to support life. Before this happens, we need to open our minds and our hearts to the lofty and freedom-furthering epoch of the Air element.

To be able to present an exercise that helps tune us to the epoch of the Air element that will govern the incoming age, I first need to make you aware of the creative power of your hands. (This is discussed at length in my book *Universe of the Human Body*. Human hands are a fractal – a holographic piece – of Gaia's creation. A gift of which humans are mostly unaware!

The four fingers stand for the four Elements and their evolutions:

— Index finger represents the Water element and the evolution of plants.
— Middle finger represents the Fire element and the evolution of animals.
— Ring finger represents the Earth element and the evolution of minerals.
— Little finger represents the Air element and human evolution.

Yet the four fingers (the four Elements) are of minimal consequence if they do not cooperate with the fifth element, represented by the thumb. The thumb represents the so-called elemental worlds of Gaia, which move her creation from within. Now we are ready for an exercise.

Gaia Touch Hand Exercise
to tune to the new epoch of the Air element

- Representing the old body of the Earth based upon the element Earth, the hands should form a closed sphere in such a way that the tips of the corresponding fingers, including the thumbs, touch each other. We have formed a closed sphere that has a one-dimensional character like the ball of the Earth seen as a material object spinning around the Sun.

- To proceed toward the new body of the Earth, which is multidimensional, we need to rotate one hand clockwise and the other counterclockwise simultaneously (the finger tips touching), until we arrive at the following finger composition: Both small fingers touch the tips of the thumbs. The other three fingers are directed toward the open space at the left and right. Instead of a closed ball representing the old space of the Earth, we have an open multidimensional structure allowing the breath of the Earth and the universe to glide through.

- The connection between the thumbs and the small fingers stands for the new driving force behind human evolution and the evolution of Gaia. The connection represents the power of consciousness (small fingers), coupled with the inspiration of the primordial — causal, archetypal — worlds of Gaia (thumbs) that move life processes upon the Earth from within.

2

The new Earth exists beyond the exclusive logical explanations

I have to admit that the above explanation concerning the present Earth Changes is purposely articulated in a logical way so that it can be relatively well digested by the rational mind. But actually, the Earth's changing process cannot be fully understood using logical explanations. The help of the right half of the brain, which symbolically stands for the intuitive and imaginative capacities of human consciousness, is inevitable. The twenty-first-century Earth Changes can be best characterized as an "upside-down process." This is one of the reasons why, parallel to sharing my logically approved insights into the process, I use the language of dreams, drawings, imaginations, and the body language of Gaia Touch exercises. Through the images deriving from my dreams and drawings, combined with corresponding hand and body movements, I hope to convey the message in a holistic way, so that both the left and the right hemispheres of consciousness get nourished. I believe that without logic/consciousness integration the new path of Gaia's evolution would not be properly embodied—embodied meaning to move with it—and there would be little chance that we could follow Earth into the twenty-second century. Perhaps we will have to leave the planet and head toward another star. Is there in our vicinity a planet of such beauty and perfection as the Earth? I doubt it.

The non-logical side of the present Earth Changes might be best conveyed by the following dream of mine from 2004:

I am riding my bicycle past an airport. Suddenly I see a dark blue airplane upside-down as it approaches the runway. I am horrified! There is about to be a serious accident! It is a passenger airplane, but I cannot decipher the name of the airline. I am on the point of phoning in the emergency but cannot remember the telephone number.

I then see a second plane landing on its back on the same runway ... and then another and another — at least twenty in all. And during all of this nothing dramatic happens. They all move past me intact and sound.

After the succession of planes, a pack of sporty looking bicyclists rides onto the runway. The riders are bent deep over their bicycles, their straining backs show intensity. Their clothing is a bright and joyful mixture of colors. Behind them march a crowd of people walking with rigidly upright posture.

I wish to emphasize that the terms "change" and- "transformation" do not appropriately describe the recent process going on with our planet. The proper term would be the alchemical idea of "transmutation," which involves the principle of "pushing something out of the established track." In this case, planes landing upside down without being destroyed is a proper symbol. The normal patterns of reality are turned on their head. For a moment one loses the ground under one's feet. The goal of the first phase of the transmutation process has been achieved.

The cyclists bent downward over their bicycles represent the second phase. They are operating their wheels like a centrifuge – a centrifuge that spews out the old and injects the new. The colorful clothing represents the earthly and cosmic powers whose positive impacts are drawn into the process.

The people marching upright behind them represent the third phase of the proceeding. They walk upright as an expression of their new identity, won through the planetary transmutation process.

The following Gaia Touch exercise may help if it is performed regularly over a period of time. It teaches the body and mind how to create a synthesis of the two brain hemispheres to combine the logical with the non-logical way of existence. The experience comes into being by rotating our hands in a circle as they touch each other continuously along their edges. Because of the specific way our body is constituted, the circle inevitably changes its form, moving the inside out. This shows that what is outside of us is simultaneously inside. Let us try:

Gaia Touch Hand Exercise
to promote the creation of the new space

- Start with open palms one next to the other, so that they touch with their edges. The tips of the fingers are directed outward.
- Now we glide along the edges of the palms without ever losing the contact between them.
- Eventually, to be able to continue we have to lift our arms so that the tips of the fingers are directed toward the inside of our body.
- Continuing with the movement, we arrive back to the initial position, where the finger tips are directed outwardly again.
- The movement is circular and can be continued as much as feels right.

The problem with logical thinking is that the rational mind is dependent on the objective over the subjective in order for the mind to function. Seeing the world and its phenomena outside of us makes it possible to understand them – yet, unfortunately, this leaves us outside of the flow of life that the phenomena embodies. Relying on objectivity as the only valid way of thinking pushes the human individual more and more into isolation from all other aspects and beings of life, including one's own self. To avoid the danger of becoming an intelligent machine, we need to rediscover our capacities for a non-logical "crazy" way of thinking. Integrating them, we should move through life in interaction with our rationally based perceptions and decisions. Both aspects of our consciousness can complement and even inspire each other.

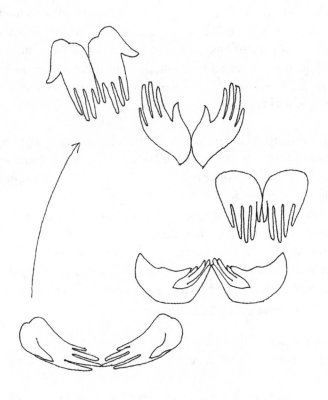

3
It is impossible to solve the emerging ecological and social challenges at only the physical level – the archetypal levels call for attention

When in Belgrade in 2008 I had a clarifying dream that the space occupied by our post-modern civilization had become too narrow to enable further holistic development of human culture. The knowledge of how to manipulate all the different aspects of living reality, often to exploit them for selfish purposes, is being perfected on a daily basis. This hits heavily the beings on parallel evolutions – the plants, animals, minerals, and microorganisms – as well as our fellow human beings, enabling suppression and exploitation. Such conditions do not allow any living being to enjoy life freely or to learn the lessons of creation that Gaia is able to teach.

> *I am driving my car on a narrow road that is loaded with traffic. I need to turn around. The operation is so demanding that I start to doubt my capacity to drive a car. A few times I bump against passing cars. Especially horrifying is the moment I strike a pedestrian. To add to my stress, the car runs out of gas. While trying to get the car started, I notice with surprise that hanging from the edge of the windshield is a line of figurines. Their forms are not quite human. My intuition whispers that if I turn around one of the figurines the car will start to move by itself. The problem is that I have no idea which of them is the appropriate one.*

The first part of the dream doesn't need further explanation. The second part is challenging. It says that instead of finding solutions to our ecological, social, and political problems in the materialized and rationally governed level of reality, we should open to the other dimensions of space and time that our modern mind ignores. These other dimensions can be referred to as archetypal or causal.

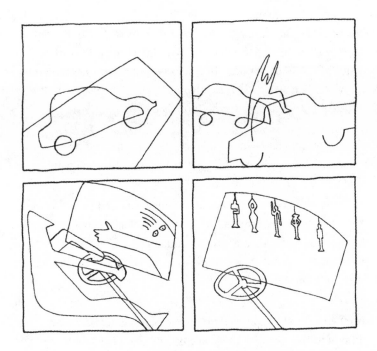

The causal levels, positioned behind manifested reality, have different laws of controlling life processes. They are revealed in the driver's intuition to ask for help from the mysterious figurines in solving the problems with the car and its engine. This intuition would be judged as nonsense by the rational mind. Yet the dream confirms that there exists a deeper level of reality where the phenomena of the manifested world are rooted in a network of archetypal patterns. Tuning to and co-operating with that level should make it possible to help the embodied world to move and evolve. Yet these archetypes — sometimes referred to as "matrices" — are not mere geometric or energetic patterns, but living beings, beings who consciously accompany the flow of life from levels of existence closer to its essence. These beings appear as figurines in our dreams due to our inability to perceive them as living beings.

What this dream conveys is that the modern human being has lost the capacity of co-creation with the causal worlds.

The following exercise can help in reconnecting with the causal dimensions, where the causes for our manifested reality pulsate. For this purpose, the exercise uses the bi-polar constitution of our body. The front of the body with its five senses is open toward the embodied world, while its backside is imagined as open to the causal half of reality, impossible to perceive through one's eyes.

- •. Sitting or standing you should create the imagination of moving backward. Make the first imaginative step back starting with the left foot and a short pause afterward.

- •. Then make a second step back in the same way, and then a third one. The exercise is more effective if the steps are done in your imagination, because in effect you are moving through several dimensions of your consciousness — but if you wish, you can also take parallel physical steps with the body.

- •. After you have done the three steps backward you should send a horizontal ray of light and love from your heart center backward toward infinity to connect with the divine background of all and everything.

- • Make a short pause again and then start to move forward. The three steps forward should be done starting always with the right foot.

- • Finally you have arrived back to your body — hopefully as a slightly different person. Take the time to feel the new quality of your being, now reconnected to the source of reality. You may need to repeat the exercise for a certain period of time to transcend the split that the modern mind has created to cut us away from the invisible worlds "behind our back."

4

The subtle powers of dragons and their life-giving breath

Folk traditions of Western cultures speak of dragons as dangerous or even bloodthirsty beings inhabiting the Earth's underground. Modern science introduced a different, even more unsympathetic view of the primeval creative powers of Gaia through its experimentation with atomic power, which has triggered terrible atomic explosions. In both cases, the reverence of the Eastern cultures for the world-creating role of dragons is missing.

The following dream from December 25, 2010, urged me to reconsider the role that dragons perform regarding the Earth and its mirroring in the human consciousness:

We have prepared a heap of dried tree limbs at the edge of our woods to be transported to our home and chopped for firewood. They are bound together in several sheaves. The truck arrives and starts to load them. Only now I realize that the tree limbs resemble dried-up dragon bodies. I watch the truck on its way toward our home — realizing that the driver has missed the right turn and is now heading in the wrong direction. I run behind the truck to stop it and suddenly find myself in a grove of beautiful trees submerged in a fairylike atmosphere. Looking around I notice, distributed among the trees, fountains spraying crystal clear water. To my surprise the fountain heads are in the obvious shape of dragon heads.

The dream awakened within me an awareness of the need to release dragons from the outdated patterns that force them into the role of monsters. But since their contribution to the creation of the Earth and the universe is not understood and appreciated by humankind in general, the will and urgency is not there to free them from these sinister images.

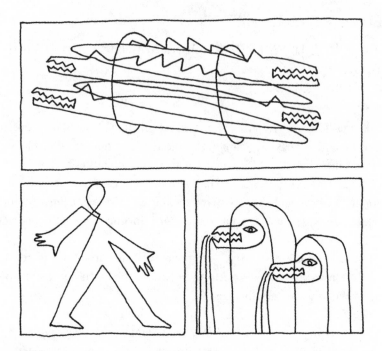

Since the dream, eight years have past. During that time I have been working almost exclusively in the field of landscape healing and have experienced innumerable encounters with the dragon presence. I have gotten to know them as silent and peaceful sources of primeval life power. Step by step, I learned that they embody the primeval creative "tools" of Gaia. They are responsible for the world we all live in. Without them, the Earth cannot exist, breathe, and be alive.

This realization is not given the proper weight as long as the human mind believes that the universe was created in a distant past either by the Big Bang or through God's hands. These beliefs are the result of rational or religious ideas and have lost the link to living reality. Reality can exist only in the present moment, the past and future are but mental concepts.

My perception of reality, coupled with my intuition, says that the space of reality is being created and simultaneously decomposed in each moment, anew at all the different levels of existence. The ebb and flow of creation is being moved by the dragon powers and directed rhythmically by Gaia consciousness. In awe I gaze upon the whole creation, including my environment, as it's decomposed, and while disappearing, composed again, always in a slightly different form. What an enormous orchestration, with the hologram of the world and its beings sliding toward zero in each moment and being already in the instant process of re-creating!

To experience the creative role of dragons one needs to descend from the macrocosmic level to the horizon of human existence. The purpose of the Gaia Touch exercise that I present next is to enable you to feel the presence and to enhance your working with the dragon power within the human body and consciousness. This exercise was originally a gift of the Swiss city of Basel. The city's name hides the presence of the bird dragon called "Basilisk." While looking at a basilisk statue in Basel, the dragon bird showed me a red point at its tail and another one at its throat. I understood that the dragon power is not only responsible for keeping us alive but is also capable of supporting human creativity—as symbolized by the throat as the source of the creative word. Later the exercise was extended to include the cosmic dragon's impact.

Gaia Touch Exercise
to connect with the inner dragon power

- While standing, reach with your hands into your back space and imitate the weaving of the dragon tail three times.
- Then bring your hands together at your coccyx to indicate the link of the dragon power with your body.
- . After a short pause, guide your hands upward along your body (touching it during the movement) until the fingers of your hands touch in front of your throat.
- While moving with your arms upward, bow your head backward to indicate the link of the dragon powers to your throat.
- While your head is bowed back and your hands are building a circle in front of your throat, you should become aware that the primeval forces of Gaia—the dragon powers—are being transformed into creative impulses.

- After some moments open your hands and stretch them out. Thereby the dragon powers can flow into the world to support the creative processes of our home planet.
- Next, the connection needs to be made with the cosmic dragon. Straighten your head and position both hands with the fingers connected slightly above the skull.
- To reach the level of the cosmic dragon you need to move with your joined hands three levels higher. Count one, two, and three.
- After reaching as high as possible, open your hands, positioning them vertically, and start to move your fingers quickly to attract the presence of the cosmic dragon.
- Now to bring the touch of the cosmic dragon down: with your hands joined, touch first your throat area and then your coccyx.
- Return to the beginning of the exercise, weaving the dragon tail. Repeat the exercise three times, and then stay for a while with your eyes closed to become aware of the experience.

As you noticed, through the exercise I have introduced the idea of cosmic dragons. I identify them as the mighty beings of the universe, the same beings that Christian theology knows as the highest rank of the angelic hierarchy: Seraphim, Cherubim, and Thrones. They are the creators of cosmic space and the universe, permeating networks of light, renewed in each succeeding moment and furthering the evolution of its star systems and their cultures. At the microcosmic level of our home planet, these angelic hosts correspond to Gaia's dragon family.

Dragons are the angels of the Earth, and angels are the dragons of the universe.

Some people may have difficulty accepting the above statement. The concept of dragons as the angels of the Earth has been hidden from Western consciousness through the use of dragon slayer myths. Germanic mythology introduced the hero Siegfried; Christian ideology, Saint George. The patriarchal societies could not occupy and govern the Earth if the primeval creative powers of Gaia were not suppressed and declared evil.

To work on transmuting the dragon slayer pattern, I use the following exercise for working both with individuals and in groups.

Gaia Touch Exercise
to transmute the dragon slayer pattern

- When you come upon a place marked by the intense presence of the dragon — it can be a mountain range or a chain of hills in the form of a dragon's back, a river or a cave — be aware of the possibility of contributing to the elimination of that life-endangering pattern.

- Make a gesture of taking a fractal (a holographic piece) of your heart quality and go with your hand (in your imagination) deep into the inside of the place to touch it to the presence of the dragon.

- Return and observe inwardly the transmutation process.

The dragon from Ljubljana Castle

5
New conditions for life are coming into existence – No Fear!

As far as we know, in the last ten millennia of human history there has never been a period when the concentration of the materialized aspect of reality has been as extreme as it is in the present. The age of the element Earth has reached its climax. The result is an extremely narrow range of reality, excluding all other dimensions of existence, especially the more subtle archetypal, spiritual, or causal. The effect of the exclusively rationalistic concept of life projected upon humanity, mainly by modern science with the economy as its obedient follower, is an outburst of interest in contemporary esoteric teachings and the spiritual traditions of ancient cultures.

Modern consciousness is trapped in an unhealthy bi-polar field, fluctuating between science and esoteric knowledge. This situation prevents the future promising processes of Gaia from creating new conditions for life. Gaia's work is being, so to say, pushed underground and not being noticed by the vast majority of the human race, and as a consequence, not being accepted and supported. At the same time, the present conditions of life upon the planet deteriorate.

The situation might be best portrayed by my dream of November 7, 2017:

I am sitting in a modern, perfectly designed airplane flying at about 30,000 feet. The pilot unexpectedly exits the cockpit, walks to the closest hatch, and starts to open it. Everyone is upset. This is a suicide! Because I sit in the row next to the door, I can see through to the outside of the plane. I see green grass! The pilot says, "I am sorry to inform you that we had to make an emergency landing." In that moment, the airplane hatch changes into an ancient, heavy, iron-bound oak sliding door. My fear is that it will not be easy to open this door.

The first image relates to the inability of modern human beings to perceive the whole of reality. The link to one's own intuition has been lost. Humankind has come to depend only on information received from official sources in the material world. As a consequence, the travelers cannot perceive the actual reality of the moment. Yet when the pilot appears in person, instead of as the expected voice from the intercom, the illusion fades. Travelers in the airplane are shown the shocking truth that instead of flying above the clouds the airplane/Earth has already landed in the new space that I call "multidimensional Earth." While we believed that we were still moving through the logical antiquated world, we have actually landed within a new, fairly unknown reality.

I see the heavy oak door as a warning that after being released from the shock of the emergency landing we won't be able simply to jump out of our materialized reality and walk upon the green grass of the new ground. The image indicates that we will have to introduce some basic changes into our way of thinking, perceiving, and creating to be able to integrate ourselves into the new space of reality.

What makes the modern human being so fearful of the new constitution of reality? To answer this question, one must first understand the source of actual material reality. The physical nature of the world is not just Gaia's creation but is overloaded with information generated by human minds and handed down from generation to generation. The fear is of an anticipated loss of stability, in effect, the loss of the accustomed mental superstructure of our environment. Although this is a valid fear, it is valid only because human beings in general have lost the ability to perceive the subtle dimensions of the causal world. These subtle dimensions will guarantee stability in the new conditions of space and time, but if one can't perceive them, it may look as though reality is crumbling.

Stability in the new conditions can be compared to standing or walking upon the watery surface of a lake or a pond. Why? The new reality of being able to integrate the subtle dimensions of existence has to be fluid and in permanent motion – but simultaneously offering stable conditions for life and its beings so that everybody can feel secure to grow, connect and be creative. This is an obviously non-logical situation that the rational mind is extremely fearful of.

Physically, it is indeed not possible to stand upon water, unless you are a saint. But if one moves attention from the physical level to the level of creative imagination – each being based upon two different capacities of consciousness – standing upon water is possible without getting wet. Let us try!

- Find a water surface, either a pond or a lake. For beginning it is better if the water surface is a calm one.
- You should imagine yourself positioned upon the water surface. It doesn't work if you imagine stepping from the shore to the water surface because then you mix two different levels of reality.
- After you have positioned yourself upon the water, you should take time to see how it feels. Then do some careful steps forward and enjoy walking upon water.

To get a feeling for the basic quality of the new space, continue the exercise either standing upon the water as proposed above or sitting at home and working through your imagination. A third possibility would be to stand at the shore of a water body such as a river, or a lake, or the ocean.

- Bow down to the water surface and perform the gesture of scooping a handful of water — without touching the water physically.
- Disperse the water into the air with a wide hands-opening gesture. Let the drops stay in the air — which means do not feel responsible for the law of gravity to act.
- Bow again and again, and continue launching water into the environment so that water drops are present everywhere in its space.
- Take a pause and listen to your feelings and intuitions.
- Imagine that there are some minute pieces of minerals distributed among the myriads of water drops around you. They make the process of materialization possible.
- Imagine that golden light beams shining from the core of Gaia reflect here and there upon the water drops. They imbue the new space with consciousness.
- Do not let the drops fall down. Rather, collect experiences of how the future and already present space of reality feels.

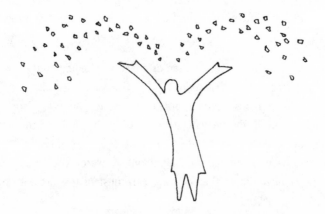

What you experienced is the sixth dimension of the new reality. It represents one of three dimensions that stand for the manifested world. Seen from this point of view, reality appears as a gigantic water sphere combined with fractals of minerals and information arriving from the heart of Gaia.

At this level, the phenomena of life do not yet take on any forms. In order for the new reality to get its proper forms, the elemental consciousness of nature needs to enter the process. Innumerable elemental beings are responsible for patterning the watery hologram and holding the focus of the forms. Then the manifested world appears knitted in its proper forms. The exercise continues:

- After you have created the watery sphere as proposed above, give attention to one of the creative centers within your body and hold the focus of your attention firmly rooted there.
- This can be the heart center, the throat, or perhaps the coccyx chakra, or the center of the perfect presence behind the navel.
- Observe the changes that follow within the hologram of the space and then give thanks to Gaia that you are allowed insights into her creation process.

Through the last exercise, we arrived at the fusion of the fourth (elemental) and sixth dimension of the new embodied reality. When it is accomplished, this fusion represents the new embodied reality that then finds its place in the fifth dimension. The fifth dimension can be considered to be a substitute for the so-called "three dimensions of the materialized world," which are usually designated as width, height and depth in the physical space.

But do not think this is the whole multidimensional space that is now in the process of becoming the carrier of the future-orientated evolution of the Earth. It is only its central part, which shamanic cultures call "the middle world." The dimensions of the cosmic "upper world" need to be added, as well as those originating at the core of Gaia – those known in the shamanic cultures worldwide as "the underworld."

In the concept of the new space that I wish to share with you (of which more explanations can be found in the Appendix) there is no hierarchical order as suggested by the shamanic tri-partite world scheme. The manifested world is at the center, while the upper- and underworld represent two different faces of the causal dimensions. The ones on the right side originate at the core of the universe and those on the left have their source at the center of the Earth.

6
Exercises of perception and communication with the worlds of nature

The secret of successful communication with beings of the living environment is a simple one: be present.

People in this age governed by rationality usually forget to be present. Constantly moving with the succession of mental patterns and social roles makes us disappear in a kind of energetic smog. Grounding in the fabric of life gets lost. Elemental beings and forest spirits complain that they can not perceive human beings because they are absent. No wonder that people cannot perceive them either. Communication between humanity and the elemental world of Gaia is broken.

Since we are working under this disadvantage, the effort to be present has to be made repeatedly. To be present means to be fully within your body – from the top of your head to the soles of your feet. You will feel it as a special quality within.

Let us say you are walking in a landscape. To be present does not mean only to be present inside your own self, but simultaneously also present within the surrounding environment. Walking in a forest for example, your soul should be fully present within the body, and also present within the sphere of your energy field, at least to a diameter of 20 yards. You should stop again and again to listen how the elemental world feels inside your field, and eventually, what it wants to communicate to you.

Next, you need to change the mental pattern that feeds your usual five-sense perception. This kind of mental pattern demands that you maintain distance from the object of interest – meaning, practically, removing yourself from the living environment that you want to experience. To change this pattern you should identify fully with the perceived aspect of reality – to be followed by translating your subtle feelings and perceptions into a logical understanding of the experience. In this way both hemispheres of consciousness take part in the perception process.

- Stand beside a tree, under its crown, imagining and sensing that the tree in front of you also stands within you. (Be sure to also take in the roots of the tree in your imaginings.)
- Be sure that the tree (within and without you) can feel your excitement about being lovingly held within your body.
- Observe what the tree within wants to show you and listen to what it wants to tell you.
- Hold your consciousness wide enough, being aware that the tree is not just within but also outside of you.

Here is another variation:

- While standing under the crown of a tree, imagine that its roots and the crown are interconnected, forming a sphere around you.
- How does it feel to stand inside the universe of a tree? Allow the tree spirit to guide you to different spaces of its tree kingdom.

If the exercises do not work for you then consider the possibility that your sequences of the perception process might be in the wrong order. To perceive the phenomena of life in their multidimensionality it is absolutely required that one's intuitive sensibility is the first to enter the perception process. Next, the intuitive hemisphere of consciousness is called into action to translate perceived vibration patterns into images, feelings, and insights. The logical mind should be the last to enter the process to read those images, feelings, etc., and formulate them into the form of logical statements.

The tragedy of the modern human being is that rational logic is allowed to jump in first as soon as one opens one's sensors to perceive a phenomenon in its entirety. Since rationality has no tools to understand these kinds of perceptions, it declares them nonsense and deletes them instantly from memory. People say: "I don't perceive anything."

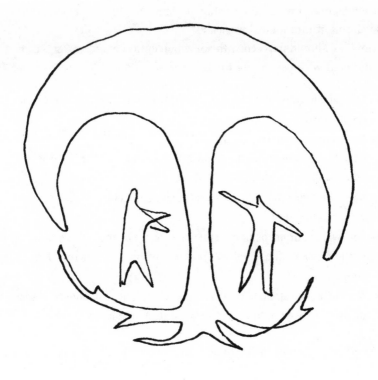

Under the crown of a tree

To achieve satisfying communication with the beings of nature the rational mind has to be held in check for a split second to allow intuition to enter with its sensitivity. In the next moment, after the successful perception, the mind can start working on the perceived material, translating it into logical messages.

Now, we should proceed with some perception exercises. Let us do an experiment with perceiving the essence of a stone.

- Standing in front of a rock, ask the stone being for permission to enter its universe.
- Be aware that entering the stone directly in front of you is not possible because you would bump into the material aspect of the stone, leaving you unhappily outside.
- Move with your attention around the stone to get the feeling of where you can enter best.
- Following your imagination, enter the sphere of the stone in a spiraling movement. The spiral will find its ending somewhere within the stone.
- Then allow the stone to show you the extensions of its "house" — some of which may be positioned outside of its material body.

Another important theme to be addressed is the objectivity of holistic perceptions.

Demanding that perception must have objective character to be of any value is a trick of rational ideology to suppress our human ability to perceive life and its beings in their entirety and their true essence. Each perception, even if the physical senses are involved, is of a subjective nature, created either within the brain cavity or in cooperation with one's imagination rooted in the heart. So-called "objectivity" is a mental concept forged in this epoch of over-enthusiasm for mechanistic rationality. Each perception is a co-creation between the concrete presence of a being or phenomenon and the consciousness of the perceiving person. Partly, it is objective, because it is related to the presence of somebody real. Partly, it is subjective, as a result of the above described perception process. Its accuracy largely depends on the ability of a person to translate the perceived light patterns into images and to interpret them accordingly.

My advice is to not bother about the objectivity of your perceptions, rather to enjoy their message and to learn from them. Be truthful and detached from ambition to perceive something that mirrors your wishes – and your perceptions will become a blessing for you and for the beings perceived. Do not hesitate to become co-creator of the new reality, which has a synergetic (subjective-objective) character, thus allowing life to flow freely between all the worlds and beings.

7
The Earth is giving birth to an age of peace and co-existence among all beings

Kranj, which is my town of birth, served in 2005 as the stage for one of my important dreams concerning the ongoing Earth Changes – Kranj is northwest of Ljubljana, the capital of the Republic of Slovenia.

The story of the dream unfolds in front of a large cave that the river Sava carved into the magnificent rock upon which my hometown stands. In 2018, while I was preparing a workshop on the urban landscape of Kranj, I had a vision making me aware that the cave had served as a place of oracle in the distant past. Pilgrims were coming there to get insights into the purpose and destiny of their incarnation. As it is usual in shamanic cultures worldwide, it was an animal spirit that took them into the inner spaces of the rock. There they were shown images that could help them to find direction in their life. In the case of that cave, the guide was the spirit of a beautiful stag. The steep road leading past that cave is even today officially called "Stag's Slope."

Because of this background story, I understand that the dream evolving in front of that cave is an oracle confirming the successful and safe outcome of the present Earth transmuting process:

As I walk down the Stag's slope toward the river Sava, I notice an old, rather ruined car positioned in front of a cave on the opposite side of the road. The driver, who is obviously heavily drunk, is asleep, leaning against the steering wheel.

A dog is lying on the rear seat howling with pain. I think to myself while walking past the scene "The driver should do something about the dog. Its life is ending. He should at least take it to the vet to get a lethal injection."

While I am saying this to myself, the drunken driver climbs out of the car, walks with uncertain steps to its rear door and bends over the dog. At that moment I realize that the dog is female and, to my amazement, giving birth to a shaggy pup.

In the next moment the mother dog opens its jaws — I am shocked — as if she were going to swallow her pup. Instead, she begins to lick it lovingly.

It is obvious that the first image of the dream portrays the actual planetary situation. The condition of the world environments is increasingly painful for the beings and families of nature. Humanity, overloaded with conflicts, poverty issues, and exaggerated abundance, is blind to the ongoing transmutation process that is essentially changing the direction of the planetary evolution.

The second image shows a surprising turning point. The driver, still half-awake and showing interest in the condition of the dog, speaks of our home planet. I link this image to the growing interest for the wellbeing of nature, its beings and their biotopes, concern about the drastic changes in the atmosphere, etc. The positive change is a result of the voluntary work of countless individuals, groups, and institutions that have started selflessly to engage in nature's protection, spreading the ideals of ecological health.

This positive trend inside the human family created the proper conditions for Gaia to start manifesting the new space and time structure that in turn opens the path toward an age of peace and co-existence among all beings evolving upon the Earth and its different dimensions of existence. The pup is about to be born.

Basically we know all this already. What needs attention are the two messages of the oracle hidden in the dreamer's reaction to the scene at the other side of the road. The first one can be found in my silent words, sounding like a death sentence, addressed to the birth-giving dog. The oracle declares that hope has to be upheld even in the moments when it seems that the world is breaking down completely. The thought pattern and the emotional attitude that the Earth is ill and life is dying blocks the possibility for the positive outcome of the Earth's transmutation process.

The second message can be read from the dreamer's fearful reaction when the mother wanted to touch her baby lovingly. The oracle says that even if extremely dramatic moments appear in the course of the Earth's changing process, we should never panic because the process and each of its sequences evolves within the loving embrace of the Divine Mother. A massive burst of fear may cause irreparable damage to the Earth's transmuting process. To be able to follow directives given by the oracle we need to train the capacity of our multidimensional heart system to hold inner peace, to hold a loving attitude toward other beings, and to fuel the quality of hope within the human psyche.

For this purpose I can offer a Gaia Touch ritual inspired by the spirit of the Swiss town of Zürich. It is based upon the power of the geometrical form called "mandorla." This almond-shaped sacred form comes about when two circles intersect: Two parent circles give birth to their divine child.

Gaia Touch Ritual
to open your multidimensional body

1. Start with your hands connected behind your coccyx, to mark the lower angle of the mandorla. This point is in resonance with the cosmic feminine called Sophia – the Wisdom from eternity. Her focus should be located behind the coccyx so that her presence arriving from the widths of the universe can permeate your whole body. Your head should be directed downward.

2. With your hands, draw the arches of the mandorla, leading them together above your head, in front of your body. The mandorla's position is a diagonal one connecting the back and the front part of the body space. Your head is now turned upward. Doing the mandorla gesture you bring the presence of Gaia, the Earth Goddess, forward so that her vibration permeates your whole body.

3. After a short pause, lower your hands, still connected, to the level of the heart. Lowering them, you create a rounded space in front of your heart, in which both dimensions are intertwined, the earthly and the cosmic, bathing in the radiation of your heart.

4. After a pause, open wide your hands to share the created quality with your environment and the world.

PART 2

Personal Aspects
of the Planetary Change

1
Gaia offers the possibility of a quantum leap in personal evolution

Throughout the millennia, philosophers and spiritual teachers have pondered the questions of human beings and the purpose of our existence. So why again question the vast body of knowledge stored in books, art, and culture? The answer is that these are clearly not normal times! Earth transformations are all encompassing, effecting not only the constitution of our planetary space but also the composition of the human being and other beings of Gaia, visible and invisible.

Forty thousand years ago human beings first appeared as Homo Sapiens. Proof of this transformational leap in evolution is revealed through surprisingly accurate animal paintings discovered in caves such as Altamira, Lascaux, etc. I believe, according to my experiences of the ongoing Earth transmutation process, that we are facing an epoch of change of similar proportion.

I would like to give logical explanations for this intuition with the help of a dream from September 1, 2016. But before telling you this fascinating story, I want to emphasize that the expected changes may need the whole third millennium to be accomplished. So there is no rush. But now, moving through the twenty-first century, the switches are being flipped – like changing railway tracks – directing our travel toward the future. We should not miss this crucial moment. What comes later will be much easier and less complicated.

The dream:

It is late at night and I am walking home, rather tired, from my work. I pass an isolated house and suddenly remember a similar moment when I was walking past this house once before, as tired as I am now. At that time, I simply went into the house, found an empty room, slept for a few hours, and then continued along my path. The inhabitants never noticed me. Alas, I decide to do the same this night.

Indeed the door is unlocked. I enter an empty room, put down my backpack, lie on the bed, and fall asleep.

I wake early in the morning, while the residents are still sleeping. It is so early that I decide not to go immediately on my way. Instead, I leave the room through the back door to sit for a moment in the garden and enjoy the early morning light.

Now I realize I should disappear before the residents awake. I need only to return to the room to take my backpack and leave. But on turning around I realize that the back of the house has three identical doors, probably leading to three separate rooms. The problem is that I do not remember through which door I entered the garden. Which door leads to my backpack?

I believe I can remember which front door I entered the night before. So I rush around the corner to look at the building's facade. Unfortunately, I find three identical front doors, with no indication which one I entered the night before.

This first part of the dream gave me deep concern. I know the human being I am: my personality, soul, and spiritual self. But then, my inability to locate my backpack and my identification documents makes it clear that this famous trinity is only one aspect of my self. The appearance of two additional doors in the dream, I intuit to mean that there are two more aspects of human identity that I know nothing about.

Luckily the dream continued, showing several symbols to help me grasp its confusing message. Throughout the following two years I have worked again and again to understand them.

While wondering which door to enter to fetch my backpack, I notice that the left door cannot be seen at all. It is hidden behind a kind of cage, woven from several layers of metal wire. The cage even has its own door. A woman comes out of this secondary door, closes it with two locks, and leaves. She is slim, tall, and shining, as if composed of light.

A small truck arrives and parks in front of the right door. Its side is open, revealing several rows of bottles positioned on shelves. In the bottles are fluids of different colors. I believe them to be different beverages like Coca Cola and some others, polluted with sugar and artificial ingredients.

The basic message of the dream is that besides the usual understanding of the human self there are two other aspects of our identity totally lost from our memory. By "usual understanding" I mean the human being as an embodying threefold self.

In the manifested world we appear as a unique personality that has a specific life span. The soul aspect denotes our identity existing beyond space and time, moving in cycles between the spiritual world of ancestors/descendants and embodied reality. The so-called "higher" self can be understood as the focus of the divine presence within the human being.

Even if difficult to understand, the dream suggests, with a strange feeling of urgency, that the other two aspects of human identity should be recognized and integrated in our lives at this particular time. My intuition says that we will desperately need them as part of our multidimensional self if we wish to pass safely through the challenges of the upcoming Earth Changes

Since the left aspect of the two forgotten faces of the human identity appeared in my dream hidden behind a metal cage and closed with two locks, it is clear that this aspect is not only forgotten but also blocked in a traumatic way. The symbol that should help to identify its essence is presented by the fairylike woman appearing out of the left door. Is there an aspect of our human self that relates to the fairy world?

The story of the dream says: "Yes!"

The fairy world is seen as a vast region of subtle beings and evolutions, of which the playful elemental beings of the Air element are only one. The Celtic culture throughout Europe, for example, knows an evolution of subtle fairylike beings evolving and creating at a specific level of the planetary space that is parallel to our own. The Celts call this kind of being Sidhe (pronounced "shee"). We will speak again about the Sidhe later, when dedicating our attention to the possible cooperation between human culture and the parallel evolutions.

Trying to identify the fairylike essence of the human being, I realize that it is not possible even to imagine. The bloodshed in the innumerable wars during the patriarchal era of the last three to five thousand years, and the suffering inflicted upon fellow human beings and other beings of life, hang heavily upon the human fairylike identity. It is indeed locked with a double lock, as it appeared in my dream. In such a case, when facing almost insolvable or even catastrophic situations, I propose to use an exercise – it is better to say a personal ritual – that I received in the pilgrimage church of the Black Madonna in Altötting, Bavaria. I call it "The Healing Tear of Grace." One collects imaginatively three drops of water that during the ritual are permeated with three aspects of healing information. The three drops are then spread over the situation or area that needs a healing impulse.

Personal Ritual of the Healing Tear of Grace

- Lift your hands in a prayer gesture to the level of your heart and let a drop of your compassion (related to the person, place, or situation concerned) fall into the space between your palms.
- Bow to the Earth, reaching with your imagination deep into the realm of Gaia, the Mother of Life. Create a vessel with your hands and ask Gaia for a drop of her forgiveness, related to the distress or insult done to the given aspect of life, place, or being(s).
- Straighten up and lift the vessel of your hands (already containing the drop of your compassion and the drop of Gaia's forgiveness) to the heavens and ask for a drop of divine grace.
- The healing water is now collected in a homeopathic way. Pour or spray the water by opening your hands, directing the healing water, in your imagination, toward its preconceived goal. The intention of your heart and the attention of your consciousness together constitute a bridge to guide the healing impulse to where it is needed.
- Give thanks. (Based on the principle of personal faith and telepathy, this ritual works over long distances.)

I ask that you do this ritual to help liberate your fairy body from the traumas of suppressing the aspect of the human self closely related to the fairy world.

Reconnecting with the above dream, I believe that it was the fairy world that donated to human beings their first body, enabling us to manifest upon the Earth and start our evolution within the beauty of Gaia's creation. This epoch is referred to in the mythologies of many ancient cultures as the "epoch of the paradise." The body that we received then was composed of water and light. Only much later did the direction of human evolution lead us deeper into incarnation, into adopting the animal body and thus being able to enter the world of matter.

Myths depict the epoch of the paradise as an epoch of harmony between all beings and dimensions of the earthly cosmos. This quality of peace and togetherness is deeply imprinted into the human fairy body – but remember that a body of this kind is not separate from our emotional, mental, and spiritual identity. At that time, body and consciousness were one.

There is a reason why our fairy identity was so cruelly suppressed in the epoch of constant wars and conscious separations. We, in fact, still experience this suppression, even if it is clothed in forms other than in the millennia before. Human beings are being prevented from remembering that an epoch of peace and coexistence is possible upon the Earth and how deeply satisfying it is. When their fairy body is suppressed it is easier to control and manipulate human individuals.

Before we close this chapter, attention needs to be paid to the second door in my dream, symbolizing another forgotten aspect of the human identity. In the multitude of bottles in the truck in front of the door were fluids of different colors. Some of them felt poisonous in a subtle way, but all appeared attractive to my eyes. They represent fluids of the human body, like blood or lymph, each separated into their own bottles and waiting to serve different bodily functions. They also serve as storage of emotional imprints and information. This is the point where contamination comes in, causing me to feel that the bodily fluids in the attractive bottles are poisoned.

Considering that we are composed of about 60 percent water, and also that water is an ideal information carrier, one can understand that our "water-body" can be overloaded with obsolete information, often with a negative connotation. This means that before touching upon one of our human identities as a water being, we need to perform a cleansing exercise of our personal ocean.

The Gaia Touch hand ritual of detachment is a gift from the spirit of a sacred tree from the island of Bali, Indonesia, where I worked on landscape healing in 2017.

Gaia Touch Hand Ritual of detachment (No. 1, Bali version)

- Hold the intention of what needs to be detached. In this case it is to detach some foreign information from our personal waters.
- Hold your hands in a horizontal position at the level of the solar plexus so that the fingers cross. Strongly press together and then released them in slow motion, taking out the polluted pattern from the personal water-body.
- Now ask for transmutation of that issue, perhaps using the violet power of change.

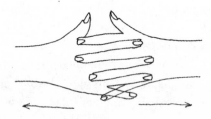

At this point on our journey of exploration of human identity, I would like to introduce another species of the Earth that is closely related to our human water-body and to the Water element. At the shore of the Adriatic Sea near the town of Piran, Slovenia, I had an encounter with dolphins. These Slovenian dolphins confirmed that we are their close relatives, and that in a distant past (perhaps during the age of Atlantis) we separated. Dolphins and whales decided to continue their evolution in the Water element; human beings in the relatively dry ambience of the Earth element. Later, attention will be given to the link between the two evolutions. At this point we need more clarity about the ocean within our individual cosmos and of its place within the holistic human identity.

Recall the exercise from the first part of our journey in which you are standing upon water and distribute drops of water throughout the environment to experience the space of reality as a hologram in water (pp. 30-31). The same exercise can be performed here, but taking water from the cavity of your belly, spread it throughout your body and beyond its physical boundaries. In this way it is possible to experience one's self as a sphere composed of innumerable water drops. The drops contain all the information needed to appear as complete human beings with fluid consciousness and forms, not fixed but in constant motion.

The incoming age of the multidimensional Earth demands from us to be able to move between different dimensions of the extended reality. While moving between worlds we will also need the ability to change body forms accordingly. The watery aspect of our identity—nowadays forgotten—is capable of fulfilling those needs perfectly.

2
The human being as a creature of the Earth – a close relative of the animals

We have looked at six facets of the human identity, and now I have to bother you with a seventh one. Only by knowing all seven facets of the human being, can one be sure to safely pass through the upcoming challenges of the Earth transmutation process. They represent different potentials of our inner strength.

I was given a hint of the importance of the animal aspect of the human being through a scientific report asserting that the genome of modern humans shares common ancestry with the genomes of all other animals on the planet (about 98% of our DNA with our closest animal relatives, the great apes). The sense of how important it would be to reconnect with the branch of our roots that touches deeply the animal kingdom was confirmed by the following dream. I had this dream while exploring several sacred places in Bavaria that are connected to the soul's path toward its incarnation in the manifested world. The dream relates to the hill of Rauhenzell, which I had visited the day before with a group of people:

I observe a breathtaking circle dance taking place inside the hill. Several animals run in a circle with some naked little children in between. The children are shouting with joy. Behind each animal a child is running trying to jump upon its shoulders. Some of them have succeeded, and I see the animals carrying them upon their neck.

Then I notice harsh obstacles upon the dancing ground. Sharp iron poles are sticking out of the ground. I am worried because the running children and animals could get injured.

Another image followed.

Now I am sitting with some adults in a boat traveling up a river. Each of us holds a passport in hand. I wonder why? During the travel, I observe the heads of my co-travelers, each of their hairstyles shows the signature of an animal body.

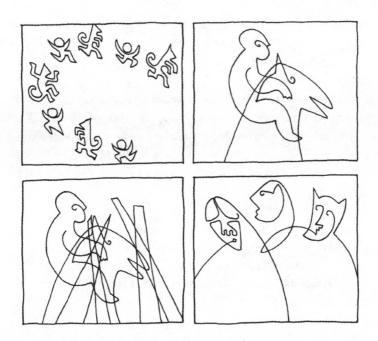

Let us enter the dream's story through the last picture. It tells us about an unrecognized fatal relationship between human beings and the higher developed animals at a primordial (archetypal) level. Members of modern civilization are usually ashamed of our obvious relationship to the animal world and try to suppress it, considering us as more highly developed beings than animals.

Each of the travelers upon the river of life holds a passport in hand as a sign of identity. To pass a border, we usually need a passport. Do the animal hairstyles indicate that animals hold the key to human beings passing the border between the spiritual world and the world of the embodied life? The first images of the dream assert the idea that during the prenatal process the soul has to connect with a specific animal species to be able to slip into a corresponding material body. Animal species, during their long evolution, developed certain models that represent the archetypal foundations of our bodily constitution. It is even possible to discern upon a person certain signs that tell us what is the related animal species.

The sharp stakes that the animals and children are forced to dance around emphasize the obstacles endangering synergy between the incoming soul and the chosen animal archetype. Ignorance of the crucial role that animals play in our life might be the most dangerous obstacle (besides the threat of genetic engineering). To work on removing this obstacle, I wish to pinpoint some precious tasks that animals perform for the ecology of Gaia. The following extract is text from the catalog of my 2018 exhibition in the Museum of Contemporary Art in Ljubljana, Slovenia: *Heavenly Beings. Neither Human nor Animal*:

> By developing internal organs that can be carried around, animals have come up with something fantastic: the freedom to roam the landscapes of the Earth. Humans have inherited the trait of being mobile from them, and have taken it in the modern age to the point of absurdity.
>
> By developing instincts, animals have paved the way for human intuition. This wonderful animal gift gives us the capacity to receive creative inspiration at any moment, be it from terrestrial or cosmic sources.
>
> Animals have developed a sense of connection and unity in flocks, herds, packs, schools, swarms, etc., so that they can live as a community. Humans have inherited this value as the capacity to create families, cultures, and societies.
>
> We have animals to thank for developing the various ways of absorbing and distributing Earth's vital force. They have taught us how to sustain life in embodied forms. Thanks to animals, the vital force can flow freely on the surface of the Earth, distributed among all living beings.

To experience the world composed of a multitude of animal species, you can use the following exercise. It is based upon the resonance bridge between the human nose and ears and the corresponding points upon the body of some mammals:

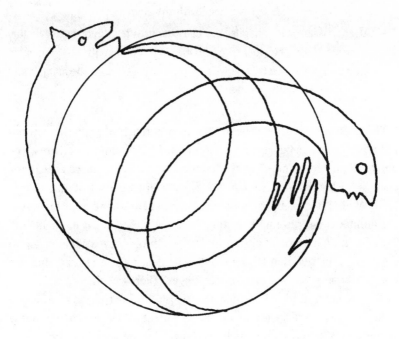

Cosmogram showing the relationship between human and animal beings, carved on a megalith in front of the Museum of Contemporary Art in Ljubljana, Slovenia

- With the fingers of one hand rub the uppermost crease of your ear. The gesture is in resonance with the pointed ears of some animals, such as wolves.
- Simultaneously rub with the other hand, circling upon the tip of your nose. The gesture is in resonance with the animal snout.
- After a while, switch hands. You can change a few times but then stay in peace to be able to perceive. One or more animals may appear in their subtle body. Gather experiences of the presence of the animals and show your sympathy to them.

There is yet another aspect of our relationship with the animal kingdom to be considered, an aspect called by shamanic cultures "the personal power animal." In this connection I wish to share an experience that I had in May 2017 in the zoological garden in Bern, Switzerland. While I was passing the large natural enclosure allotted to a lynx, the animal came running past the fence and gazed for a moment into my eyes. In that moment a tiny fly dropped into my eye. While trying to get it out, I realized that the seeming coincidence was a message that we humans have forgotten our animal selves. There was incredible power in that message, and also a hidden proposal on how to work on experiencing the animal inside as our inner potential. Its presence is today anchored inside our bone structures, especially the vessel of our hips as the carrier of important vital functions:

- Sit or stand in peace. Be aware of the bones of your hips and rub them with your hands for a while.
- At the right moment your attention should jump from the hips to the breast bone. Rub your breast bone for a while with both hands.
- Then the spark of your attention should jump to the area of the subtle bone structures that underlay your nose, eyes, mouth, and ears.
- Take some time to observe inwardly what feelings and images come up and what message from your power animal may appear. Do not allow yourself to be blocked by the idea of a fixed power animal that you may consider to be your own. Be open to the message of the moment.

The following Gaia Touch personal ritual honors our human relationship with the animal kingdom, making us aware that the power animal, in effect, represents our own inner potentials. Finally, the boundary between the human being and its inner animal is nothing else but a mental fiction:

Gaia Touch Personal Ritual
to connect with your inner animal

- Stand upright with your feet positioned in the following unusual manner: with heels spread as widely apart as possible and the big toes touching. In this position direct your attention to the causal level pulsating "behind your back"—in effect, to the causal level of your body where the animal is present within your body.
- Positioning the feet like this, you allow your knees to touch. Knees symbolize a relationship that has the character of a family. They are in resonance with the world of the ancestors and descendants as well as with the other relatives of the human race, which includes the animal world.
- Such a position of your feet and knees forces you to lean forward and creates the image of the animal body, which is of a horizontal nature.
- While you are leaning horizontally, only the animal's front legs are missing. Bring both of your hands forward over your shoulders and stay in that a position for a while in order to come in resonance with your inner animal.
- Then change to the clear vertical body posture that is characteristic for the human being. Your knees go apart, but the feet remain in the awkward position. Through this change you have absorbed the animal to become part of your human identity.
- Finally, bring the position of your feet back to normal. Doing this, your hands go backward, so that you stand in the light of the moment as an incarnated human being with the animal aspect integrated.
- Give thanks to the animal kingdom for the gift of your incarnation.

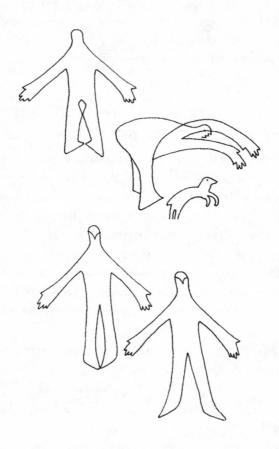

3
The elemental self of the human being in relation to our spiritual self

Examining the fairylike identity of the human being and our fluid, dolphin-related aspect does not end our interest in the multidimensional human identity. I would like to bring attention now to what my daughter Ajra called the elemental self of the human being. We need to touch upon the identity of the human being as a being of the earthly universe, our "green" aspect.

Monotheistic religions try to convince us that we are only casual visitors on the Earth and that our true home is in the spiritual realms. The atheist's approach to life is similar, but atheism does not offer any after-death refuge. As a result, the modern human attitude toward the Earth in general is a negative one, ignoring the value of Gaia as a place where humanity is offered the ideal conditions to evolve as a race of loving and creative people and to enjoy life in its fascinating embodied form.

To be able to continue the journey with Gaia we need to recognize that our cooperation with her has a deep spiritual value, both for furthering our personal evolution and as the evolution of her creation. Our companionship with Gaia has had a very long history, during which, parallel with developing our spiritual identity, we became beings of the Earth, not much different from animals, elemental beings, plants, and stones. The elemental self is a manifestation of our creative long-term involvement with the evolution of the earthly universe and its beings.

How can we understand the elemental self in relation to our spiritual aspect, which is usually called the soul? The soul is a subtle being composed of light frequencies. It knows a binary rhythm of existence.

In one leg of this rhythm our soul exists for a period in the subtle landscapes of the earthly universe known as the realm of the ancestors and descendants. One can imagine these as immaterial landscapes and cities composed of light and positioned on either inside the mineral layers of the planet, in its atmosphere, or in the depths of the oceans.

In the second leg of its existence, the soul takes a rather complicated path, embodied in a material form and living among stones, plants, animals and fellow human beings. After the embodied phase is concluded, the soul, of course, needs to return along a similar path back to the realm of the ancestors/descendants to continue its evolution there.

This brief overview of the continuously repeating binary cycle of the soul is needed to pinpoint the moment when the soul again and again meets its elemental self.

The elemental self is not composed of light frequencies as is the soul, rather it consists of atomic and sub-atomic particles that originate in the realm of the dragons, the primeval creative organs of Gaia. This is why the elemental self, being a daughter or son of the dragon, is capable of creating conditions for the soul to be embodied in manifested form within its emotional, mental, and etheric layers, and finally in the material layer. The soul – our spiritual self – and the elemental self are like twins. To be able to live life embodied, the soul, in one of its prenatal phases, has to fuse with its counterpart, the elemental self.

Unlike the soul, the elemental self does not abide in the realms of light between two incarnations but exists immersed within the plasma of life – better to say – it is part of the fabric of life, composed of different intertwined layers of micro- and nano-beings. Partly they can be identified as units of Gaia consciousness, partly as microorganisms, and partly as cosmic inspiration bearers. Later we will attend more fully to the plasma of life. It can be imagined now as a river of life flowing through all beings and extensions of the embodied world, making us all alive anew in each moment.

Similarly, in the same way that our spiritual self has three extensions, mentioned in the previous chapter, the elemental self also can be seen as threefold:

- The elemental self in its role as earthly sister/brother of the soul embodies the identity of the individual human as part of nature, as part of the evolution of the earthly universe, and as a unique creation of Gaia.

Interaction between the individual soul and the elemental self

- The second layer of the elemental self is called the personal elemental being. It is a subtle being of nature's consciousness spread throughout the liquid areas of our body. Its task is to facilitate the perfect functioning of the body organs and extensions.
- The third layer is called the personal elemental master. It represents a fractal of Gaia pulsating within the embodied human being and contains the divine wisdom of the Earth soul. The role of the personal elemental master is to inspire the human being to evolve toward becoming co-creator with Gaia, working on developing the Earth as a place of peace, reconciliation, and incomparable beauty.

After the individual human beings have concluded their journey through their life span, the two aspects of their identity separate step by step. As mentioned, the soul abides in the realms of the spiritual world, while the elemental self dissolves into the plasma of life and enjoys its "after-death" period distributed among plants, birds, stones, and other elemental worlds. In the moment when the corresponding soul starts again its descent upon the manifested plane of the Earth, the elemental self begins to gather its sub-elemental particles and to focus itself for the new joint venture, traveling with its sister soul through the marvels and challenges of the embodied world.

This is a nice logical explanation to satisfy the mind. In effect, the spiritual self and its elemental counterpart never separate completely. There exists always a resonance bridge between them that can be activated in each moment. Using the resonance bridge the soul can in any moment appear through some natural phenomena. This is why indigenous cultures, through different signs in nature, can read messages of their ancestors or descendants. Seen from the other side, the deceased can contact their original communities or individuals they feel deeply connected to, using natural phenomena. This way they can stay relatively close to their beloved ones even after they have left the plane of manifested life. A bird coming again and again to tap upon the same window could be an example. Or a deer crossing your path at a particular moment or the sudden appearance of a breeze. Objects fall sometimes to the ground in such a way that there is no logical explanation for their movement. Your intuition will tell you to be alert and to look for the meaning of this message. It may be "simply" a call to stay in touch or to reconnect.

Better not to wait until one dies! It is important to develop a deep connection with the elemental plasma of nature while we are walking amidst its embodied beauty. This helps us also to reconnect with our own elemental self, thus strengthening our bonds with Gaia and her creation. This will be of decisive importance in the approaching rough times of Earth Changes. The soul may get lost in certain upheavals but your inner elemental master will know the way.

Also be aware that through modern "high-tech" technologies human civilization heavily drains the plasma of life, thus reducing the possibility that human beings can appear in the world in their entirety, and not as "organic" robots but as someone connected to the essence of life and its beings, both visible and invisible.

I propose next an exercise to connect to the plasma of life and to experience its different aspects:

- Be present, possibly in a place in nature. Imagine that the world around you is not in a condensed state, but getting more and more permeable, so that drops of water, cells, particles of minerals, and such, float freely in the space.

- Your body loses its distinct forms, and its particles becoming freely suspended in the space. Take time to construct this imagination and then gather experiences of yourself as being part of the elemental plasma of life.

- What holds all your particles together, so that you don't get lost in the river of life, is the radiation of your "fixed star," the heart center. You can see the gold-green radiation of your heart mirrored upon the particles of your presence. Be aware that your presence at this level is not separated from nature's environment. Enjoy being part of the plasma of life.

Gaia Touch Ritual
to connect with the three aspects of the elemental self

- Fold your hands in a praying gesture and reach above your head backward toward the point on your backbone located between the shoulder blades. This is the focus of the elemental self. Now make a pause to connect.

- With the prayer gesture go across the central axis of your head and body down to the level of your heart, keeping in touch with your head, with your face, your throat and the center of your breast. Pause at your heart center to connect to the wisdom of the elemental master.

- There, turn the prayer gesture upside down to touch your solar plexus area with your fingertips as the focus of your personal elemental being.

- After a short pause, perform a rounded gesture around your body with the tips of your forefingers touching, to declare yourself as a member of the large circle of Gaia's elemental world.

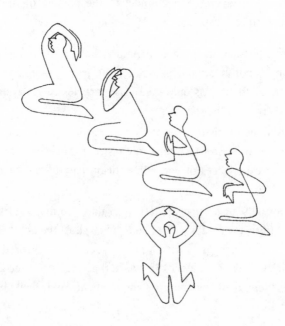

4
Cooperation with the inner dragon is inevitable

I am not introducing here another aspect of the human self. With the inner dragon, one is dealing with such a vast amount of power and consciousness that it cannot be condensed into an individual body—even if that body is a multidimensional organism much vaster than the material structure. Although we are not capable of experiencing the full power of Gaia's primeval powers, in this chapter I hope to introduce you to some ways of recognizing and experiencing the dragon presence around and also within us.

I believe that to be able to face the challenges of the approaching Earth Changes, it is necessary to recognize and accept working with the dragon power within. I was moved to explore the relationship between the individual human and the dragon presence in the following dream:

I see a girl lying powerless on the ground. She seems to be very ill. Without hesitating, I lift her into the back of my Jeep. But before leaving for the hospital, I decided to take a gas mask with me. My intuition says that on the way I may encounter difficult situations requiring the mask. At the beginning I leave the mask hanging around my neck, but later I decide to put it on. Looking at myself in the rear view mirror, I am surprised to see that the gas mask has several illogical extensions that make my face look like that of a dragon.

To decipher the message in the dream, I propose that the powerless girl and the dragonlike driver are the same person. The girl represents the modern human being, burned-out by the social and ecological pressures of contemporary life. Existing social and political relationships demand for us to function exclusively at the rational level, removing us from the loving touch of the heart. Further, the ruling elites have invented methods to spread fear among the population through planned or invented

terrorist attacks and economic pressures. At the same time, the future of life on the planet, from an ecological standpoint, is uncertain.

The driver, with his protective dragon mask, looks in the mirror to find the strongest remedy for solving the problems torturing the modern human being. Instead of looking for solutions outside of one's self, one should find access within to the lost source of healing potentials, wisdom, and peace embodied by the dragon powers of Gaia.

Easy to say, but as mentioned before, the full forces of the dragon are far stronger than can be harnessed within one's self. These forces hold the atoms of matter together. The immensity of these forces is displayed in an atomic explosion when the energy of just a few atoms is released.

So how does one open a path of cooperation with the world of the dragon without being consumed by its immense forces? First, it needs to be stressed that dragon wisdom and power alone cannot bring direct solutions to day-to-day problems. Its precious role is to activate beings and energies of change that are bearers of helping strategies. Secondly, the dragon power as consciousness and energy is too strong to find its permanent home within the human body. To be able to develop a cooperative relationship with the dragon, we should invite its touch into our body (see pp. 23-24).

I wish also to express my opinion here that certain kundalini exercises that aim to further spiritual capacities of an individual through the use of dragon powers are not necessarily for the good of the whole.

Further, one needs to bear in mind that dragon powers pulsate beyond space and time structures, and beyond the realms of the manifested world. Yet they know ways to touch embodied levels of existence and corresponding beings to unleash intense processes of change and inner growth. Words are not sufficient to describe those paths. It is best to experience the creative presence of the primary creative powers of Gaia directly.

This is the purpose of the following exercise. It accentuates the cavity of the belly as the region that can be brought in resonance with the dragon powers that are present within Gaia's creation everywhere. Through this resonance they can also extend their presence within the human body to bring their special gifts to our life and creativity.

- State clearly within your heart and mind the reason you invite the dragon power to become creative within your world. Beware selfish purposes!
- Be aware of the belly cavity (bowl of the hips) as a resonance space where the presence of the dragon can resonate with its power and wisdom.
- Imagine the chalice of your belly cavity as made from glass or precious metal to resemble the Tibetan singing bowls. This is to support the resonance bridge that you will activate next.
- Imagine the presence of the dragon, in the form of its breath, spiraling throughout the belly region, rubbing against the walls of your "singing bowl." Listen to the sound, color, energy that comes into existence.
- Guide the colors, sounds, energies emanating from the bowl as vivid streams toward the anticipated goal, embracing and permeating it.
- If you wish to purify your environment or a certain situation, color the streams with violet, to raise the vital quality of a place color them green. The color white supports the quality of purity, etc. In addition to the use of color, always add a touch of gold to honor the presence of the dragon.
- Do not forget to give thanks.

Cosmogram dedicated to the fire dragon

5
Dynamite in our personal luggage – overheated yang and other challenges

The last chapters helped us appreciate the richness of the human self, suggesting innumerable possibilities for inner growth, creativity, and the bringing of joy to other beings. Unfortunately, most of these gifts stay blocked as mere potential – even when the individual is aware of their existence – because of the useless baggage that people unknowingly carry along their path. Either we do not know of the destructive patterns that we protectively carry in our bodies, or we are blocked by fear from the traumatic knots submerged in our subconscious.

A dream from autumn 2018 emphasized the imperative of continuing the work of emptying my internal baggage. I will tell this story because it is clever in characterizing the three aspects of "personal luggage" that should be dealt with before entering the more intense phases of the Earth transmutation process.

We have just arrived on a bus at the bus station. I need to run with my luggage across the street to the railway station to catch a train. The time to catch the train is rather short, so I hurry to leave the bus. But I am surprised when the driver stops me just as I am ready to jump through the open front door. He tells me that my wife is calling with a message for me – my cell phone is off. To identify me, the driver asked my wife: "Do you mean the man carrying an enormously thick book under his arm?" I tell him that I haven't the time to talk to my wife because I need to find my luggage and hurry to the railway station.

This prologue is the framework within which the message of the dream evolves later. We learn that a big change is approaching that demands that we be alert and ready. The voice of Gaia talking to the driver accentuates the unnecessary luggage that we need to rid ourselves of if we wish to embark upon the train to the future Earth. The enormously thick book, which I am not even aware I am carrying, is a symbol to be unraveled.

I run to find my luggage, leaving my wife on the phone, waiting. Meanwhile, our suitcases are unloaded and lined up so that everybody can find his or her own. I run up and down the line but cannot find mine. Then, I remember, I borrowed the suitcase from a stranger, and now I am not able to remember what it looks like.

Working later on to decode the dream, I realized that my first interpretation for not finding the suitcase was false. In effect, the suitcase stands for one of the most traumatic experiences of my life, and I had been suppressing that memory out of fear. Later, in my imagination, I identified the suitcase and opened it. A completely black, hairy little boy jumped from the empty suitcase into my arms. This was a lost piece of my soul that had been deeply traumatized during a six-month quarantine I was forced to endure as a five year old, when I was infected with diphtheria. I temporarily lost my ability to speak and didn't even recognize my parents when they came to fetch me from the hospital.

While searching for my suitcase, I feel a strong desire to know when my train will depart—to be clear about how much time I have at my disposal before the approaching change. I notice that I am carrying a long box with all kinds of train timetables. Looking at them, I discover that they are all out of date. I am aware that in my wallet I have a piece of paper with the actual timetable, but my sense of urgency precludes taking my wallet out to look at the train's departure time.

The language of the dream is very clear in this sequence. In the age of the Internet we have access to an enormous amount of information. But like the papers in my box, they all refer to the past because they do not know the law of the present moment. The dream states clearly that human beings could know the purpose of their life and the "timetable" of their actual incarnation. It is written in the memory of our causal body. But instead of listening inwardly, we mostly orientate ourselves according to the governing ideologies, thought patterns, and superficial information.

The dream continues with the story of the thick book:

I feel a great resistance to taking it with me, but I know that it belongs to me and I am obliged to take it. I originally found it on the floor in a kind of large fenced-in space. To my surprise each of the travelers from the bus has a book lying there, not just me. They are of different sizes, and mine appears extremely thick. I feel a strong wish to get rid of it but cannot find a place to leave it.

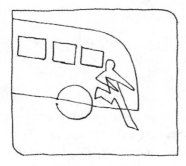
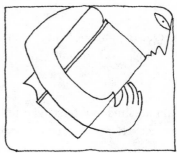

Working with the image of the book in a meditative way, I found that it is similar to a dictionary. Innumerable phrases that refer to different links were printed into the intercellular spaces of the human body at the atomic and subatomic levels. This is a guide to a region of our body's memory, memory positioned deep in our subconsciousness. One can imagine it as a level where atoms combine to create cells, also as the level where the dragon powers operate.

The links created at that level influence, to a certain extent, our consciousness and, consequently, our activities — be it for the good or bad. If those links are tuned to the actual development of the Earth and the universe and to the spiritual purpose of an individual's life, then they attract supportive powers and inspirations from the cosmic environment. If those intercellular links are a reproduction of past patterns that have lost relationship to the present moment and are out of tune with the actual phase in the evolution of the Earth and the universe, then they hinder the spiritual development of individuals and represent a hindering agent in their life and creativity.

There is one kind of hindering intercellular link that comes into existence if certain dogmatic ideas are imprinted into the memory of an individual from one incarnation to another. I can give some examples:

- that masculine dominance over feminine qualities represents a natural or even cosmic law. During several thousand years of patriarchal rule, most human cultures have developed under this fixed idea.
- that physically manifested space is the only true reality.
- that the human being is superior and should rule over all other beings of the manifested world.

The list goes on!

Another kind of intercellular link with negative results for our lives is of exclusively personal origin. Traumatic fears or ideological prejudices leave deep imprints at the sub-elemental levels. There are also traces of unresolved tragedies from past lives. Broken, long-standing relationships may also leave unredeemed traces. And so on...

My practice is to be alert and notice when unusual situations appear in everyday life, especially if they repeat themselves, following a certain rhythm. They often represent coded messages urging us to make order in our cellar. Dreams can be of great help in detecting the dynamite hidden in our personal luggage. Trust your inner voice and trust your helpers and allies at the different levels of existence. They will make you aware of the patterns you have outgrown, hidden traumas, or intercellular links that at the appropriate moment need to be transmuted and detached from your individual world. Ask your spiritual guides for help.

In the case of outgrown or even destructive patterns, you can use the Gaia Touch hand ritual of detachment that I received on Bali (p. 50). In the above dream, those patterns are symbolized by the box with useless timetables. They are imprinted on the rather superficial, emotional, or mental levels.

Traumatic knots are represented in the above dream by the seemingly lost suitcase. This kind of "dynamite in our luggage" demands to be dealt with. The personal ritual of the Healing Tear of Grace (p. 48) can be of great help, and also the Dragon Ritual (pp. 23-24).

The above dream also points to the existence of a third level of problematic luggage. The thick book of intercellular links, carried under the arm of the dreamer, demands my awareness. Yet, when I tried to reach the extremely deep level where the links exist, I felt hopeless – until the Canal Grande in Venice offered help with the proposal of a useful hand ritual.

The Canal Grande ritual is rooted in the unique structure of the canal, which forms the reverse of a letter "S". The two semi-circles of the "S" are plus/minus polarized. At the point where the two extremes meet, the famous Rialto Bridge links them, holding the balance between the earthly and cosmic halves of the Canal Grande. This relates also to the planetary balance in general. The spiritual function of the Rialto Bridge has been intensified because for over 600 years it was the only bridge arching the Canal Grande. (Another bridge was built in 1856.)

Here is the exercise:

- Position your hands in front of your chest. The thumbs and index fingers of both hands touch each other in a circular form so that both circles are intertwined. The circles are now in resonance with both semi-circles of the Canal Grande and the point of intertwining resonates with the Rialto Bridge.

The above exercise developed later into two different aspects of the Canal Grande ritual. The first one is to release the outdated connections at the intercellular level; the second is to create fresh connections opening toward the future.

Gaia Touch Ritual to delete outdated links and create new links at the intercellular level

- Start by deleting outdated information. While holding the above-described link between the thumbs and the index fingers, release the connection 5 times, making the distance between the thumbs and index fingers as wide as possible. Do this 5 times to relate to all the five elements: Water, Fire, Earth, Air, and their (etheric) causal level.

- After you have done the detachment with your index fingers, do it also with the other three fingers in the same way. The deleting of the useless sub-elemental connection is accomplished.

- Now you will need to proceed with an exercise for transmuting the leftover energy of the deleted link. For this you can radiate violet light from the center of your hands – the color violet is the color of transmutation.

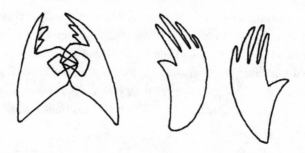

The exercise continues by creating a renewed connection that is in tune with the present cosmic moment:

- The "positive" (constructive) aspect of the Canal Grande ritual on p. 73 starts by holding the connection between your thumbs and index fingers, but this time you will also release the link, creating for a moment a space between the thumbs and the index fingers.

- Immediately after you have released the link between the two fingers, spin the left hand to the left and the right hand to the right. In the next moment, touch the thumbs and the index fingers again. The link between them is re-done, *but on the opposite side!*
- Reverse the motion of your hands, taking them back to their original position.
- Repeat the process five times, and then remain silent for observation.
- Proceed with the other three fingers. one after the other, always re-linking in the same way.

If you want to be sure that the new subatomic links you created are in tune with the new space of reality, then before starting to recreate the connections, you can perform (a few times) the Gaia Touch ritual of tuning to the new epoch of the Air element (p. 13).

6

Listen to the voice of your inner self and speak with the voice of your heart

Through the current Earth Changes we are approaching the threshold of a unique cosmic portal. It offers to everybody the freedom to decide what one's own personal and, consequently, the global future will be like. We can certainly continue moving upon the existing tracks of evolution, but be aware that, under the condition of rapidly deteriorating environments, social tensions, and political frictions, it is uncertain where our civilization will land.

In this guide I am making an alternative path through the rather complicated situations ahead, following a different approach based upon the wisdom and power of love. I have the intention to find a way that leads through the cataclysms – not ignoring them – toward the age of peace and creative freedom. Do not think that I am a fantasizer!

I dare to make such a statement because during the last two decades I have witnessed an unexpected revelation of the power and wisdom of love. Different dimensions of what is usually called "the heart chakra" opened one after the other. Instead of a single heart center, I had to recognize the existence of a complete "heart system" that can encompass the whole human being if its importance to the meaning of life is recognized.

Step by step I discovered a complete geomantic system pulsating within the whole of the human body and being. I call it "geomantic" because it is similar to vital-energy systems permeating the landscapes and oceans of the Earth.

Based upon my own experience, I believe that the loving system of the heart can lift us as human beings to another level of existence, to enable us "to go through the fire without being burned." I can say that other beings of the manifested universe look upon the human being as the potential holder of the key to opening that love-based creative dimension for all while we are facing the unpredictable Earth Changes.

The revelation of the holistic heart system started at the goal of the famous pilgrimage path at Santiago de Compostela, Spain. Arriving at the cathedral and passing the overloaded Baroque facade, I lifted my gaze toward the ancient figure of the Christ positioned over the original portal from the Roman era. Immediately I realized that the Christ figure is not blessing the arriving pilgrims in a usual way. Instead he is demonstrating the gesture of the opening of the heart center. I see his hands with open palms move apart, touching his body all the way backward.

When I repeated the gesture upon my body, I realize that the capacity to radiate into the world with the power of love increases. It increases even more if I perform the gesture very very slowly, observing and feeling the different qualities of love that open up and start to radiate. This is how the first sequence of the Gaia Touch body ritual to open the heart was born. It can be used as a ritual even if it does not relate yet to the complete heart system:

Gaia Touch Body Ritual to open your heart system – short version

- Keep your hands held upward in front of your heart center in a praying gesture.
- When you are ready, start opening your hands very slowly, like a door opening.
- When you arrive with the back side of your hands at your chest, and when you cannot take them any farther, continue opening the door in your imagination until the two sides are swung open completely to the back.
- Now the light of your heart shines freely into the world, to bless life inside and around you.
- This ritual is finished by going back to the initial prayer gesture in front of your heart center, which is both a thanksgiving and a closing the door.

It took several years, often performing the ritual with different geo-mantic groups, until I got to know the back aspect of the heart system. Then I changed the ritual to using the back path of both hands to open the back side of the heart center.

In *Universe of the Human Body*, I explain in detail the meaning of the causal heart system focused at the back of the heart chakra. I present the front aspect of the heart center as a cluster of heart micro-centers embodying different qualities of love. They can be experienced through the above Gaia Touch ritual if the opening of the heart front aspect is performed very slowly and followed by intuitive perception. Their task is to bring different shades of love into the world.

The back side of the heart center can be imagined as a cluster of tiny stars. They contain archetypal qualities of the cosmic love. Their task is to feed the human capacity to love by anchoring different aspects of the universal heart at the causal area of the human body.

One can imagine the cooperation of the back and the front aspects of the human heart system in the form of a lemniscate (a figure-8), the symbol of infinity. The front loop of the lemniscate, encompassing the cluster of the heart centers, opens toward the manifested world. The back loop refers to the mentioned constellation of mini-stars. What is usually called "the heart chakra" appears at the point where the two loops of the figure-8 cross. The crossing represents an interdimensional portal that

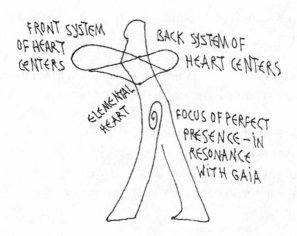

enables communication between the heart micro-centers operating in the manifested world and those focused at the back. This is why the heart chakra appears as the source of the heart qualities, even if they can exist only if both clusters communicate with each other. As a result of the continuing revelation of the heart system, the ritual developed further:

Gaia Touch Body Ritual to open your heart system—longer version

- Hold your hands in front of your heart center to form the praying gesture.
- When you are ready, start opening your hands very slowly, like a door opening. Carefully move the hands as closely along the chest as is possible.
- Make a short pause when you cannot move your hands any farther. Now the light of the cluster of your heart centers shines freely into the world to bless life inside and around you.
- By slowly going back toward the initial prayer gesture, you open yourself to the back system of the heart.
- While moving the arms forward lift them to the horizontal level so that opening the back space is more accentuated.
- Try to feel the precious focuses of the universal love at your back.
- The closing prayer gesture of the ritual should be used as a gesture of thanksgiving.

During the last few years, this Gaia Touch ritual has been complemented with several new aspects. Before integrating them into the ritual, I wish to mention them:

- We have already given attention to the elemental heart. It represents a holographic piece or fractal of the heart of the Earth present within each human being.
- Through the center of the elemental heart, positioned at the lower end of the breastbone, we enter the heart system of Gaia. It permeates the landscapes of the Earth and is present as a microform within each of us as well as within each being of nature.

- The region of our personal dragon is focused in the chalice of the hips. This forms the root of the heart system anchored in the belly, and it gives the love impulses of the heart the strength to overcome all possible obstacles and to reach as far as intended.
- The throat area of the body is included to support the creative faculties of love.
- Lastly, the hands find their place in the Gaia Touch ritual to awaken the full love-sharing potentials of the human heart system. The hands symbolize the will to put love impulses into action in the situations of everyday life.

Gaia Touch Body Ritual
to open your heart system — complete version

- Go with your hands deep down into the region of your belly to connect with the personal dragon, representing the roots of the heart system. Position your arms so that they to touch each other back to back. Your hands also touch back to back.
- Start to lift your arms to the level marked by the lower end of the breastbone, to connect with the elemental heart. While lifting your arms, they have to be turned around to their normal position. Your hands should form a chalice in front of the elemental heart.
- Move your hands three times in and out, similar to the beating of the heart muscle. (The tips of the fingers are still aiming downward!)
- Lift your hands to the traditional prayer position to touch the area of the heart center.
- After a short pause, start opening your hands very slowly, like a door opening. Move your hands as closely along the chest as possible.
- Make a short pause when you cannot move your hands any farther. Now the light of the cluster of your heart center shines freely into the world to bless life inside and around you.
- Slowly going back to the initial prayer gesture, start to open the back system of the heart, which is ready for the inspiration of cosmic love.

- Make a short pause to feel the existence of the precious focus of the universal love at your back.
- While moving forward, lift your arms to the horizontal level so that opening the back space is more accentuated.
- You have now returned to the praying gesture in front of your heart center. Lift this praying gesture until you touch your throat with the tips of your fingers. This is to support the creative aspect of the heart.
- Open your arms diagonally to make clear your intention to put love into practice through the action of your hands.
- Get back to the prayer gesture in front of your heart and continue the ritual in the opposite order: open the heart in front and then in the back, go down to the elemental heart, pulsating the elemental heart three times, and finally go down to the depth of the belly region in the way you did in the beginning. The cycle is finished. Repeat it possibly two times more.

7

Exercises to walk the path of life in the attitude of a pilgrimage

I suppose that the day might be close when we will have to step out of our cars and learn to walk along our life's path. The time is ripe to learn how to walk in the way to arrive closer to one's own essence. For aboriginal cultures, walking upon the Earth represents one of the most important everyday rituals. For them, touching the Earth by walking — especially barefoot — means to be constantly in touch with Gaia, the Mother of Life.

Using walking rituals in the epoch of the upcoming age of the Air element has a basically different meaning. The Earth is not only under our feet, not only around us embodied in the beauty of the natural environment. Gaia is now becoming present within our consciousness as our co-creative partner.

No doubt, our body identifies with Gaia's body, similar to all other natural phenomena that are united with her. But with us there comes into being another quality of relationship; one that knows the hitherto unknown synergy between the body and consciousness.

I hope that the following walking exercises will make the unique relationship between the body of the Earth and human consciousness more clear.

Here is my first proposal:

- While walking, imagine being accompanied by a red point that moves with you about seven inches below your feet. This point represents the deepest focus of our chakra system, connecting the human being with the core of the Earth.

- Stop here and there, and take the experience that develops during your walking into your heart to become aware of its quality. Go on walking after a short pause, and continue this rhythm.

Another interesting possibility is to walk in a similar way, but imagine carrying with you a green point between your knees. Knees easily resonate with the world of the ancestors and descendants.

Complementary to these two proposals is walking with a golden point above your head, positioned as high as your hands can reach. This can be done along a passage with ancient trees on either side or along the central axis of a Gothic cathedral.

The following way of walking can help you to come in touch with your personal elemental self. (Remember clarifying the relationship between the soul-spiritual and the elemental aspects of the human being, p. 64):

- While walking, imagine that a child is walking with you. His shoulders are not higher than your knees. Through this kind of walking, a binary rhythm comes into being. As you take one step, the child must take several smaller steps to keep up with you. This binary rhythm of walking comes into resonance with the binary rhythm of the soul cycle in relation to the cycle of the elemental self.

- Stop here and there to feel the quality that develops within you. Each stop may bring to your consciousness another aspect of the relationship to your elemental sister or brother.

Another method of walking brings one close to the causal worlds positioned behind the body:

- While walking, stop here and there to take three steps backward. The steps backward should be started always with the left foot and with the awareness that you are approaching the "black cave" of the primordial world.

- After taking the three steps backward, pause to become aware of the experience.

- Continue walking, then stop, cautiously take three steps backward again.

It is very enjoyable to celebrate such walking rituals with a group. Someone from the group should have the task of making a sound to signal when to switch from experiencing back to walking.

The following group ritual can be used to encounter deeper levels of a place and to experience its underworld. (Only the group spirit is strong enough to enter the inside of a mountain, for example.)

- . The group stands in front of a cave, close to a mountain slope or a rock wall.
- Facing the wall, ask for permission to enter the underground. Then physically walk in place as a group, without moving from the place.
- After a while the group leader makes an audible signal to stop "walking." This signals the group to focus on the experience.
- Another signal follows, and the group starts again to walk in place, etc.
- . Several sequences of this should be done. Then pull some rational thoughts into your awareness, and you are out of the underground. Give thanks.

There are some other walking exercises connected with the number of steps. They can be performed either physically using your legs or simply through the imagination, and they can be performed either individually or in a group.

- To experience the watery ambience of a place you should first do 4 steps backward and then 6 steps forward.
- The steps should be done individually so that their number can be clearly imprinted into the universal memory. Go forward with the right foot and backward with the left.
- Make a pause and ponder the experience — in effect, allow it to slowly ascend into your awareness. Then repeat the exercise a few times to intensify the experience.
- To experience the presence of the primordial dragon powers within you, do the exercise with 2 steps forward and 8 steps backward.

Walking exercises are also important for our grounding. But grounding principles are changing. The past method of grounding by imagining yourself as a tree with roots anchoring deep in the Earth can result in a dramatic temporary personal loss of grounding. It holds the individual too tightly tied to the ground. In this epoch of great changes we need to be flexible, capable of moving at any moment, like a fox.

And yet, in these changing conditions human beings need to be grounded, not flying around in illusions. The following meditation gives a more effective way of horizontal grounding:

- Imagine that your body is connected to the different facets and elements of your living environment with the help of innumerable tiny threads equipped with sensors at their end. Through the sensitivity of these threads the body receives, every moment, the information important for its stability in space and time.

The following exercise combines a grounding exercise with walking in a natural environment:

- In this walking exercise we use the chakras of the soles of the feet. Imagine that the center of the sole of each foot is the source of radiation that is creating two spheres around your feet. Be aware that these chakras represent a sacred relationship between your body and the core of Gaia.
- While you walk the two spheres merge partly with the ground upon which you are walking.
- There is always one foot that connects to the Earth and one that is free. This binary rhythm of being linked to the earth with one foot and a free being of the Air element with the other, alternating with each step, is a way to be grounded and also to be able to move with the changing Earth.
- Pause here and there for a while, taking the experience into your heart to experience the new way of being linked to Gaia.

At this point I would like to present a chakra system that I have brought forward in many of my books. It has a feminine character in contrast to the hierarchical order of the classical seven-chakra system that supports the masculine domination over our culture.

This new chakra system begins by focusing on the chakras of the Air element. They are positioned in the middle of the soles of our feet, and they are paired with the two located at the center of our palms. In the Christian tradition they are called stigmata, but in effect, they belong to the circular chakra system related to the five elements.

The five-element feminine chakra system is focused in the heart center, which represents the element of Ethers as the Fifth element. The first circle of the chakra system is in resonance with the Water element, the next is in resonance with the Fire element. With the element of Earth, one needs to stand up with the hands and feet stretched out. The Earth element chakras are behind the elbows and behind the knees. The outermost circle is in resonance with the Air element with the chakras positioned in the middle of the foot soles and at the center of the palms.

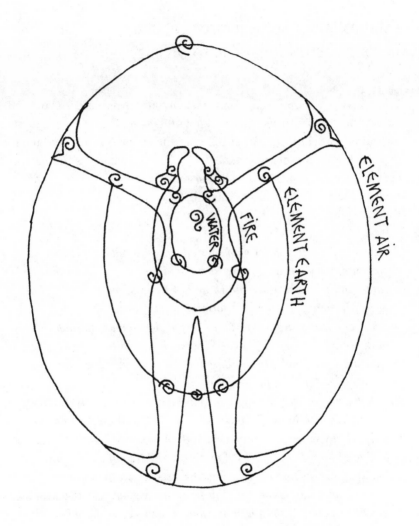

The five-element feminine chakra system

8
Establishing a non-hierarchical and beyond-institutional link to Divinity

When giving a name to the universal Divinity, I purposely avoid the expression "God" because I wish to honor its feminine face, equal to its masculine one. But this is not the only theme concerning the human relationship to the divine realm that calls for change in the present epoch. The present-day hierarchical institutional link to Divinity is not in tune with our age of change. This might be best communicated by the following dream of mine from October 16, 2016:

I am standing at a point above a highway observing a permanent stream of passing cars. To my surprise, I notice among all these cars a tall white carriage pulled by two pairs of white horses. I ask myself if there is a circus performing in our town.

The carriage takes a turn and stops at the side of the road. It parks so close to me that I can observe it in details. The carriage is guided by, seemingly, two children, a boy and a girl, but according to my feelings, they are fully adults.

A voice says that the carriage will be in my town only for today.

Standing in a kind of large basket at the top of the carriage the girl and boy make a gesture of invitation permeated with a deep feeling of love. It is addressed to all the children of the town, inviting them to come onto the strange basket-like platform.

A boy with dark skin comes in first. Surprisingly his two hosts know his name. Calling him by name, they receive him with the feeling of overwhelming love.

I notice that the carriage is wrapped in thin, almost invisible foil.

My three small daughters have also heard the call and come running to the stairs leading to the platform. The oldest one climbs to the top while the other two stay upon the stairs, hesitating. I am uncomfortable with their hesitation.

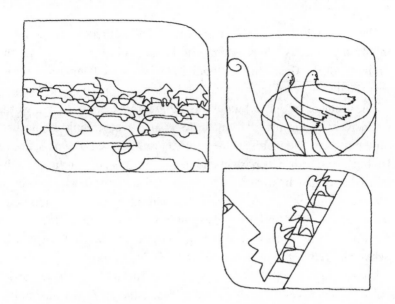

Printed in my memory is the indescribably deep feeling of love emanating from both masters of the carriage. Secondly, considering that they are at the same time children and adults, one can suppose that they exist in the timeless sphere, so to say, in eternity. Also their carriage appearing among the crowd of cars as a unique phenomenon painted in radiating white allows us to identify them as representatives of the universal Divinity. The nearly invisible foil wrapping their carriage supports this interpretation. It points to the sphere of the Divinity as belonging to a dimension that, even if fully present, cannot be perceived by the human senses.

If you can imagine that the adult girl and boy stand for the Divinity and their carriage for the realm of the divine presence, then we have the key to what is new on that exalted level of existence.

First, I would like to point to the presence of the divine carriage in the middle of the car traffic. This symbol speaks to the present relationship between the Earth and the divine dimension of the universe. Divinity no longer abides in the heavens, but is now incarnated upon the Earth, right in the middle of the havoc created by modern human culture.

The tragedy is that the divine presence is still not recognized as being involved in Earth's nature realms and human culture, even though the Prologue of the Gospel of Saint John almost two millennia ago stated that the divine Word incarnated and dwelt among people.

The problem is that religious institutions bind Saint John's words exclusively to the incarnation of Jesus at the beginning of the first millennia A.D. The words of the Prologue suggest that the presence of Divinity on Earth is a past phenomenon, as other monotheistic religions have also held their avatars attached to the past ages, be it Moses or Muhammad. Are religions afraid of losing their dominance over nations if the Divinity, persisting in its demand for righteousness and for the loving care of all beings, visible and invisible, would be acknowledged in the present?

My dream is very clear in this respect. The white carriage carries the representatives of Divinity right among the modern cars – not in the past, but now – even though the car drivers, each in their own machine, might believe that they are driving past a carriage belonging to a visiting circus.

Further, I find most important that Divinity in the above dream presents itself as balanced in its feminine and masculine aspects. Modern spiritual movements based upon the Christian tradition usually call them Sophia and Christ. Buddhists would recognize them as Tara and Buddha. In my dream, they both radiated the same quality of cosmic love, so that I experienced them almost as one and the same being.

Next I wish to emphasize that the divine couple did not call any adults to come onto their platform. Their call was exclusively directed to children. Why? My understanding is that children in relation to adults stand for the soul aspect of the human being. The birth of a child brings to the relatively problematic reality of the manifested life the subtle and pure breath of the soul. This means that the call of Divinity to reconnect with its essence at this particular moment in time does not touch the bodily aspect of people, but their soul aspect.

Even if people relate to different religious traditions or are atheists, they are invited right now to answer the call of the universal Divinity.

But what is the purpose of that call? Since human beings are addressed in their soul aspect, and not as personalities driving their cars, I interpret that the purpose is to make people remember why they decided to incarnate in this specific age and how important it is in the given circumstances to connect at the soul level to the divine dimension of existence, usually called "the spiritual world."

The spiritual world should not be confused with the world of the ancestors and descendants. The world of the ancestors and descendants exists at subtle etheric levels as diverse realms where human beings in their soul aspect abide in the time between two embodiments on the Earth. The spiritual world belongs to a cosmic dimension of existence. It can be understood as the higher self of humanity, composed of highly evolved humans and other beings that hold upright the divine vision for the development of the human race and its involvement in the evolution of Gaia and her worlds of nature and culture.

Considering the spiritual world, do we speak of Divinity as one? Yes, but it has simultaneously two aspects – the feminine and masculine – and exists at the same time also as a multitude of divine beings representing the whole spectrum of the spiritual world.

Finally, we also need to give attention to the voice in the dream stating that the carriage will be in town only today. The immediacy of the event finds an echo in the concern of the dreamer for his two daughters who hesitate at the base of the stairs leading to the divine platform. I interpret this sequence as a warning that the time is ripe to make a decision at the soul level to be willing to contribute one's individual share to the Earth transmutation process, so that the future of life and its beings will be secure even if apocalyptic times may come upon us.

To repeat, the call is not addressed to the people driving in the shells of their cars. Many of them are not awake enough to make such a decision right now, and yet the dream confirms that for the reason of the safe development of the Earth Changes, the decision should be made now, even if they are not ready yet to express it at a fully conscious level and through their own activity. At the moment it is enough to be aware of your soul's decision, which is carried in the heart, and perhaps to express it in a symbolic form through a self-composed prayer of dedication in a personal or group ritual.

Also you can make a silent decision under the star of your soul:

- Imagine sitting under the night sky with innumerable tiny stars.
- There is one especially bright star shining high up behind your back. You cannot see it. It is the star of your soul.
- Imagine being lifted to a certain level toward that star. Express your decision silently.
- Staying there, touch the ground to create wide and deep roots inside the body of Gaia.

In this way, you can experience yourself as inhabiting the vast body of your soul. Remember that you do not need to die to reconnect with your soul body. It walks with you along your earthly path.

PART 3

Transmutation of the Earth and Human Culture

1

Possibilities of a relatively peaceful planetary change

I cannot promise that moving through the Earth Changes will be free from the challenge of a cataclysm. Climatologists predict the collapse of the planetary life systems if strict measures of atmospheric protections are not started immediately, but it is obvious that there is not the political will to undertake these changes at this time. However, in a complex dream that I received in 2013 there was the message that a relatively peaceful transformation was still possible.

Under present conditions can we still open to the message of that dream? Let's be open for a miracle! There is no possibility of a peaceful planetary change without taking measures to transform the message into a realistic possibility.

The dream is composed of two parts, with an intermission between:

I must give a lecture at 4 o'clock in Trbovlje, Slovenia, a town at least two hours away from Kranj – my hometown. The friend who will drive me there points out that it is five minutes to four. I am panicked because I will be terribly late, but I tell the driver that I must first run home and change my clothes to be properly dressed for the lecture. I must also find my late father and give him the keys to my home. The clock shows 4 o'clock when I return to the car. The situation is so painful that I awake.

The first part of the dream paints the dramatic situation predicted by climatologists followed by their urgent call to immediately change our habits related to the use of fossil fuels, or it will be too late. Collapse of the life systems will have unpredictable consequences for all the beings of the Earth. Often the phrase "5 minutes before 12 is mentioned" meaning that, in effect, we are already too late to take measures.

My wife awoke at the same time and told me about the dream that she had simultaneously with mine. She saw a bright electronic screen with the numbers 4 and 16 endlessly repeating. I understood it immediately. The lecture was not at 4 o'clock/4.00 hours but at 4 o'clock/16.00 hours. I felt relieved. I had 12 hours more to prepare for the lecture in Trbovlje.

I intuited my wife's dream as an indication that the science predicting rapid deterioration of the Earth's biosphere was in a different time scale than the one related to the actual Earth transmutation process. The scientific predictions were based upon a level of evolution that was no longer relevant since Gaia was closing the evolutionary path related to the element Earth. The "timetable" of the Air element is already valid – as explained at the very beginning of this book. We are called upon to be optimistic and hopeful, even though the predicted cataclysmic events for nature and society seem inevitable.

Then, I fell back to sleep to dream the following in a duet with my wife:

Since I now have 12 hours at my disposal before the lecture starts, I decide to visit town "Y" on the tramway. I intend to take the line leading to town "X," change trams and continue to town "Y." This path would form the letter "V."

During the ride to "X" the tram passes a building similar to a church. Its facade is adorned with a large relief. At the left and right the figures of the Divine Mother and Divine Father are sculpted. In the middle between them stands their Son. I notice that his heart center is wide open. Attracted by its radiation, I look through the Son's heart center. Behind his heart I see a celestial garden with blooming lawns and dark green cypresses. I see Gaia as the goddess of the paradise, and also the Sun and the Moon.

This vision inspires me to make a quick decision to change tram lines at the next station. This shortcut changes my path from that of a "V" to more like the bottom half of an "A." Following this path, I will not need to go all the way down to "X" at all. Using the short cut, I will have more time at my disposal for the visit to town "Y".

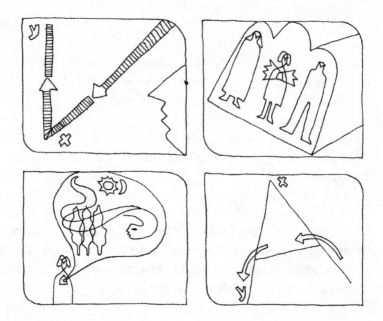

The second part of the dream brings awareness of the possibility of avoiding the final crash of the life systems of the Earth. The key to understanding the message can be found in the transformation of the path taken by the Earth Changes from the form similar to the letter "V" into the one symbolized by the letter "A." Such a transformation, as shown in the form of the letters, means in effect turning the situation upside down!

The letter "V" symbolizes the predicted unfolding of the Earth Changes as following two phases. In the first phase the path leads into a valley of increasing destruction of the planetary biosphere and its final break down. The natural catastrophes we have been experiencing in the last decades are part of this downward path. After the lowest point is reached, the transformation path could turn around and slowly start to rise, following the second side of the "V," and bringing the first signs of planetary recovery. The way up would probably require many ages to restore the present beauty of the planet – if that would even be possible.

If the process followed the "A-path" model, then the prospects for the future would be much more optimistic. Using the shortcut along the horizontal line of the "A," the hellish final destruction of the planet would be avoided. The required transmutation of the planetary space and human culture could still be fulfilled. In the language of the dream, 12 hours would be gained to allow the slowing of the path of transmutation. People who at the moment have lost themselves in illusions of multiple kinds could have the time to recognize and join the path to the new age of peace and cooperation among all the beings of the earthly universe.

The key to understanding the method for achieving this optimistic change was inspired by the facade of the sacred building in the dream. The two enormously tall, stone grey figures, I interpret as representing the divine couple that inspired human evolution. The Father figure can be identified as the God in the Heavens adored by the patriarchal religions. The Mother figure represents the Mother of Life, who was held most sacred worldwide in the aboriginal spirituality. They appear to be withdrawing. The Son, in the middle, is alive, shining from his heart. He embodies the newly revealed matrix of the future human being, free from the patriarchal patterns, and also free to develop a different relationship to Gaia, the Mother of Life, because humankind's childhood has passed. It is time to become fully responsible to Gaia's Creation.

The window to the heart that the Son opens to the dreamer clarifies the direction we need to move in order to create new relationships between the human race and Gaia. The obvious solution is to engage the loving consciousness of our hearts, as the dreamer did when he decided to change to a different path to avoid the destruction of the planet. What messages are hidden in the background of this informative dream?

The dream tells us of three conditions that will enable us make a contribution to the prevention of what could possibly be the full destruction of the Earth:

- We hold anchored within our hearts the vision of Earth as a sacred garden of Gaia in which all worlds, beings, and powers cooperate in harmony, mutual respect, and co-creative joy. The vision from the Son's heart is valid and should be nourished within ourselves, even though we are bombarded with the reality of permanent wars, fake political leaders, and the destruction of the natural environment.

- We are not emotionally overwhelmed and obsessed by the life-threatening waves of the incoming Earth Changes. Instead, we should search for, discover, and support the existing path of Gaia. Gaia, together with her elemental and spiritual helpers, is already on a planetary transmutation path toward the avoidance of a final cataclysm that would permanently threaten the breathtaking beauty of planet Earth.

- As adult daughters and sons of Gaia, we become co-creators of the transformation that our home planet is going through. As consciousness embodied in matter, many human beings have already demonstrated — through street protests demanding measures for the protection of nature, by adopting a recycling economy, etc. — their decision to renounce the path of destruction. Yet, the decision has little value if it is not consciously supporting Gaia's plan to remodel the complete space of the Earth with the aim to become a garden of creative peace.

The following chapters will touch upon different possibilities of how to help the decision for life to become a fully functioning reality.

2
Advantages of cooperating with parallel evolutions — dolphins, Sidhe, and Ents

To understand the possibility of cooperating with beings belonging to parallel evolutions in the prevention of the collapse of the Earth's biosphere, the rational model presenting the Earth as simply a single sphere needs to be abolished. By "single sphere," I mean the material body of the planet as seen from satellites and experienced through our physical senses. It exists as such, certainly, but rational perception cannot understand that the materialized Earth sphere is just one of a group of spheres that comprise what I call "the earthly universe."

Besides the physical sphere (our sphere that is shared with plants, animals, and minerals), all the other spheres are of a subtle nature and therefore not visible with the physical eyes. Each of these invisible spheres is the home of another evolution that takes part in Gaia's universe. The first part of the book, for example, mentions the fairy world of the Sidhe. The Sidhe world, an invisible world, represents an organism as equally complex as our physical Earth. The evolution of the dolphins and whales can also be imagined as existing within an autonomous world sphere. The same can be said about the world sphere of the ancestors and descendants. And there are certainly more spheres within the cluster of Gaia's cosmos. Each of them can be imagined as existing within a different vibrational spectrum. This provides the environment necessary for the vital and spiritual evolution of these diverse beings, enabling them to also fully enjoy Gaia's hospitality.

I call the composition of Earth's spheres "a cluster" because they are not each isolated in their own void. Constantly moving, they intersect at different points, creating the possibilities for the individual worlds of Gaia's cosmos to communicate and cooperate with one another.

I am aware that the image I have portrayed looks rather mechanistic, because it is missing the center. The center holds the cluster of worlds together as a unit and allows the fluidity of movement necessary for constant communication with one another. The "Sun" that gives light and inspiration to the cluster to exist and to evolve is the Earth's Divinity and the cluster's creator – "Gaia."

Now the scene is set to bring attention to some of the units taking part in the Earth's cluster of related autonomous worlds. To start, let us examine briefly the world of dolphins and whales. Since I do not have enough experiences with whales, my story relates to dolphins.

My initiation into the world sphere of dolphins happened in 2010, during a concert dedicated to the dolphins and whales, performed by the duo "White canvas." The concert had just begun when, to my surprise, an unknown folk presented themselves to my inner eye. Similar to a chorus of singers, they stood upright in rows upon a levitating black platform. Because they had fish tails instead of feet and radiated an innocent childlike vibration, my intuition identified them with the evolution of dolphins. The black platform suspended in the air showed me that they do not belong to "our" Earth's sphere.

Later during the concert, they presented themselves as riding upon dolphins – an image that I know from ancient Roman art. But they

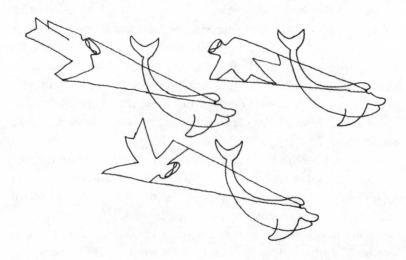

corrected that image to help me to understand that, in effect, they are incarnated within the fish-like dolphin body, looking through its eyes into the manifested world of Gaia. Like human beings, who are able to enjoy life incarnated through cooperation with the animal world, they cooperate with the fish body of dolphins and whales to the same effect. This explains their amazing intelligence, what some people recognize as the healing power of dolphins, and the exquisite opus of whale songs in the depths of the ocean.

When working on landscape healing with a group in the area of the Costa del Sol in southern Spain, we arrived at the large bay of Algeciras on the coast of the Atlantic Ocean. It is said that the dolphins go there en masse to mate. My perception was that their priority for the journey was to connect with their cosmic homeland, which can be imagined as an ocean existing in some other corner of our galaxy.

When I tuned to the dolphin presence there, a number of dolphins in their subtle bodies jumped into my embrace. I asked them to show me an exercise through which I could tune in to the presence of their consciousness. Here is the exercise they proposed:

Gaia Touch Personal Ritual
to connect with the world of the dolphins

- Stand upright with your heels touching each other. Then open your feet as widely as possible to create the image of a dolphin's tail.
- Then, the front fins come into action. Position your hands so that they form a triangle in front of your heart center.
- Open and close the triangle few times, as if wagging your front fins. The movement represents simultaneously opening your loving heart.
- Now, you enter the dolphin's sphere of consciousness. Stand normally, and start with perception of their world or go into dialogue with them.

I have performed this ritual often, with different groups, even when we were not at a seashore. It can be done at any water body, even a river or a pond. It does not matter. The dolphin presence appears

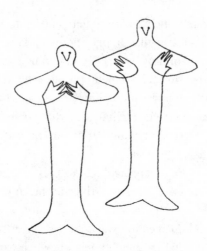

immediately. I learned that dolphins share among themselves a global network of cosmic consciousness. With this ritual you can tune into their network, wherever you are, and take part in the pulsation of their exquisite wisdom and love.

Another spherical world of the Earth's cluster that has expressed the will to collaborate with human culture to avoid planetary catastrophe is the fairy world of the Sidhe.

During the last eight years I have had several encounters with the Sidhe world. One of the most interesting happened upon a half-deserted island called Torcello in the lagoon of Venice.

In the middle of the first millennium A.D., Torcello was a flourishing town and the center of the lagoon (Venice itself did not exist yet). But so much of the earth's matter was deposited in that part of the lagoon from the Alpine rivers that by the end of the 8th century commercial boats could no longer approach Torcello. The leader of the lagoon's republics, Doge Angelo Partecipazio, decided in 810 A.D. to transfer the whole city to the place of the today's Venice. Houses and palaces were deconstructed and brought by boat to the area of the present center of Venice, around the Rialto Bridge, where they were rebuilt. But they did not dare to move two sacred buildings, the former Cathedral of Santa Maria Assunta and the hexagonal building of Santa Fosca, which still stand in the middle of the otherwise nearly deserted island. The canals are still there, but not the houses and palaces that surrounded them.

Instead, another city is flourishing there today, the invisible city of the fairy civilization of the Sidhe. Besides a few houses serving the visiting tourists, Torcello seems empty, but when one leaves the single tourist path that leads to the two churches and tunes to the sphere of the Sidhe, then the communication can begin.

During my visit to Torcello at the beginning of 2019, I learned some basic information to assist in understanding the essence of the Sidhe evolution and to prepare to meet and communicate with the Sidhe light.

It is clear that Sidhe evolution has its source in the great universe, as do the races of the dolphins and the human beings. The Sidhe woman with whom David Spangler had dialogues, which were published in his book *Conversations with the Sidhe,* confirms this clearly. But how does it happen that they can exist within the Earth's cluster? In order to exist in the conditions of the Earth, dolphins and whales adopted the fish body. Humans needed almost ten million years to adopt the body of the primates. What about the Sidhe?

I was told on this occasion that for their purpose they were allowed to adopt the body of elemental beings. This sounds logical. That elemental beings or nature spirits are invisible does not mean that they do not have bodies. To work within the fabric of nature, their bodies are made of subtle substance. By adopting the body of elemental beings, Sidhe exist as invisible beings. This condition is relatively recent. Legends describe elemental beings in past ages, before rational logic began to dominate human consciousness, as being semi-visible. Such a relationship with human culture might also be true for the Sidhe.

It was also made clear that being co-creators with Gaia and relatives of the elemental beings made it possible for the Sidhe to develop technology that can affect physical situations upon the Earth in a very practical way. As elemental beings are creative in forming and nourishing the manifested life of nature – plants, animals, minerals and human beings – the Sidhe beings are able to co-create to heal conditions in the physical world, even though their technology is not of a physical nature. They can create by reaching from the etheric into material levels of the earthly universe. Consequently, they could help if the physical conditions of the planet were to spin out of control.

Further, I found that the Sidhe have a different relationship than we do with the life of nature. As subtle beings, they connect with a subelemental level of nature, in other words, to the causal background of manifested nature and landscape. Working creatively from that level of existence, they could prevent the breakdown of natural life systems in the event of cataclysmic conditions caused by the Earth Changes.

I was also made aware of a special link connecting the Sidhe folk to the world of the dragons. I was given insight into a feminine dragon that they safeguard, a white dragoness, embodying the wisdom and the powerful love of Gaia. They protect this white dragoness from the devastating mental pattern of the killer dragon that is projected by our human patriarchal culture.

The following Gaia Touch body ritual to help connect with the sphere of the Sidhe comes from a visit to a stronghold of their culture, Pieve di Soligo, Italy. The ritual refers to the threefold organization of the Sidhe world, which is similar to the classical shamanic world image. The middle world is described through the aspects presented above. The upper world is the home of the Sidhe elders that hold the connection to their interstellar source. The underworld is a kind of hatchery where the future Sidhe are being raised, similar to larva in the insect world.

Gaia Touch Body Ritual
to connect with the world of the Sidhe

- Stand with your feet as much apart as needed to secure your stability. Open your hands diagonally to greet the fairy world of the Sidhe.
- Bring the right arm in an arch to the left side, to position the right hand upon the left one, leaning with the body as much as possible to the left side. (The drawing shows the figure from the back.)
- Bring the right arm in an arch back to the right side, as if to open the space in front of you. Now you stand again with open hands, as in the beginning.

- Then bring the left arm to the right side to position the left hand upon the right one, leaning with the body as much as possible to the right side.
- Now to touch the Sidhe underworld. To accomplish this you should bring joined hands in a downward arch from right to the left. The downward arch should pass the level of the knees.
- When bringing the right arm to the right side, while the left one stays on the left side, both hands are open diagonally as at the beginning of the exercise.
- Repeat a few times fluidly, and stay for a while with closed eyes to feel the quality of the Sidhe world.

A third parallel evolution and another precious ally are the Ents, beings inhabiting some of the oldest and wisest trees. They should not be confused with the tree spirits called "fauns" in the Latin tradition. Fauns are elemental beings of such subtle bodies that they can permeate trees to guide their growth and the enfolding of their task in the given ambience. Ents are not elemental beings. Their home is in another star system, yet a part of them, embodied in an older tree, collaborates with Gaia.

Their name comes from Tolkien's *Lord of the Rings*. There, Ents appear as spirits inhabiting ancient tress and as the saviors of humankind. When the forces of darkness were about to destroy the human race, the Ents came to stamp down the kingdom of evil with their immense power.

One of my first encounters with Ents occurred a decade ago at an oak tree that was planted at the beginning of the nineteenth century in Leipzig, Germany, in the memory of a victory over Napoleon. Approaching the mighty tree I felt a command from the oak to kneel down close to its trunk. Kneeling, I saw a thin little figure dancing permanently inside the tree trunk. It was a foot high and seems to be composed of a fluid blend of shining metals. I felt an immense power emanating from this tiny figure.

The next meeting of interest with an Ent happened in the company of a group of geomancy students, while exploring an oak in the vicinity of Bad Blumau, Styria, in southern Austria. This oak is considered the oldest oak of Europe. Its presence was documented a millennia ago. At first, I was aware of only the tree spirit, the faun, permeating the tree. Only later did I become aware of another presence inside the trunk, which was extremely luminous, like lightning. I dared to ask: "Who are you?" The answer was: "We are like you. You are embodied in the outer universe of the Earth; we inhabit the inwardly turned (outside-in) space of the trees."

Two aspects seem important in this statement. First, Ents are an evolution of the same rank as the human one—a cosmic evolution joining the Earth systems as a guest of Gaia. Second, they inhabit one of the spheres composing the cluster of Gaia's worlds that touches the sphere of the manifested world through some of the special trees existing upon the Earth.

My next encounter with an Ent brought me more clarity about their origin. It came while I was tuning to an ancient rubber tree in the Botanical Garden of Rio de Janeiro. This time I saw the Ent sitting inside a royal, red-colored chamber within the tree trunk. I felt the sacredness of its presence. The feeling was accompanied by the words: "Coming from a mighty, distant star, we exist in the state of nirvana, permanently connected to our star's presence" and by a scene around the center of that star. Thin channels reached out of the star, resembling umbilical cords. Attached to the end of each of these cords, I saw an Ent. I then understood how this relatively tiny being could radiate such tremendous power. The full power of that star vibrates through each of the Ents.

In autumn 2018, while exploring Central Park in Manhattan, I found in the northern part of the park an old maple tree covered with astonishing knobs on its trunk. My intuition pointed to an Ent sitting inside. I asked him to propose an exercise through which it would be possible to experience the presence of Ents. The following exercise was his proposal:

Exercise to connect with the world of the Ents

- Stand in front of an old tree that you feel could be home to an Ent.
- Bow down, and imagine reaching under your feet with your fingers.
- Remain for a while like this. Then stand up, imagining that your hands stay under your feet. This means that your hands and fingers are now much longer.
- To achieve the proper proportion between your hands and your body, you need to grow to the stature of a giant. Now you are ready to perceive the Ent, or feel its presence within the tree. Your body, as a giant, corresponds to the immense cosmic power concentrated in the Ents.

You might be disappointed because the practical aspects of cooperation with the subtle allies of the human race are not yet formulated. This is not possible and also not needed yet. We first need to get to know each other and build bridges of communication. Without first learning to inwardly touch each other's presence the outer forms of collaboration are not possible.

3
The culture of exchange with the plant world – animals retreating

I have mentioned a few times the close relationship between the embodied human race and the animal kingdom. It is undeniable, but it needs to be said that in the face of the oncoming Earth Changes this relationship may have to change drastically.

The animals are living their lives according to their matrix, which is unfortunately deeply disturbed by the present human civilization. There is no question that change is needed and inevitable. The tragedy is that human culture in adopting certain aspects of animal culture has perverted and misused normal animal behaviors ad absurdum. Shedding blood in wars, terrorist actions, the way we feed ourselves by abusing other beings as part of our human economy, are examples of this misappropriation.

A future era of peace and co-existence is possible if human culture would move from animal-like foundations to vegan ones. I certainly do not mean only in the way we feed ourselves, but the ways in which we mistreat each other and others of Gaia's kingdoms. I want to say that plants offer a different kind of example for human culture, so that it can be rebuilt in tune with the complete cluster of Gaia's universe. One could call it "Gaia-culture," "Gea-culture," "Geo-culture." This kind of vegan foundation already exists within us. We do not walk upon four legs, but stand upright like a stalk of grain or an apple tree.

The following dream supported me while I was contemplating this directional change:

I come to an exhibition looking at different models of family homes. My surprise is enormous! All the houses are positioned on the top of the living boughs of trees! A casual observer says to me to look more closely at the houses to the right. I realize that they are made of thick grey material, like army tents. They have some *torn edges, and floors that cut them off from the tree crown below. Then an enthusiastic voice says: "but look at Plato's house!"**

Looking to the left, I see a tree crown with a house positioned on it that is made from thin parachute silk of numerous vivid colors. Its sides are fluttering in the wind. The dark green tree leaves are its floor.

Then I notice a group of young men standing upon the ground. In their hands they hold up wands with living plants fastened at the tops. Two of the men make me aware that their plant wands are touching each other as if waves of conversation are running between them.

---

*("Plato's house" refers to the house of the future. The Greek philosopher Plato presented a consciousness that appeared rational in its clarity of thinking but was still connected to the wisdom of eternity.)

First, the dream makes us aware that the idea of human culture as separate from nature is nonsense. Even if at first glance it appears crazy to see houses positioned upon the soft and succulent tree leaves, with a deeper look, it makes sense. The trees in the dream stand for the creative breath of Gaia, with its source at the divine core of the planet. It flows from there through the realms of nature – also represented by the trees – to finally unite with the larger universe of the solar system.

Human culture, at the tree crowns, is at the proper and optimal place, with human dwellings and human creativity perfectly nourished by the rising breath of the Mother of Life. In the opposite direction, the tree leaves take in radiation from the cosmos – the sun rays – so that human culture, symbolically positioned upon the tree tops, is also bathed by the whole spectrum of the cosmic powers and qualities.

This is the ideal picture. The dream also gives us the sad portrayal of our actual situation, where the human dwellings are made of thick grey army-tent material, with a solid floor that cuts them off from the tree crown below and consequently from the exchange of life power and wisdom between the Earth and the universe. The dreamer also notices that some edges of the tents are damaged, indicating the fraying of modern civilization.

"Plato's house," an alternative to this dull image, is presented to the dreamer in a vision of the future development of human culture. Plato's house has no fixed floor and instead is open for the exchange between the microcosm of the Earth and the macrocosm of the universe. The tree's green and succulent leaves make up its floor. The house dancing with the wind can be understood as being in tune with the Air element as the guiding element of the future evolution of the Earth's cluster of worlds. The freedom to dance with the wind symbolizes the freedom of the coming era of the Air element. Through the Earth Changes, all the obstacles preventing free expression of the inner truth – for human and other beings – will be removed one by one, allowing us all to be who we truly are and to create our joyful contribution to the beauty of life. The colors with which Plato's house is permeated help us to remember that consciousness in the era of the Air element should not to be understood as mental consciousness, but as consciousness permeated by the whole spectrum of loving emotion.

The young men with plants on their wands are a depiction of the transformation of society, running parallel to the changes in human culture. In this case, "small" plants are the focus, not the trees. That they are "planted" upon sticks and held in human hands, not in the soil, is demonstrating something specific to the human world. Touching each other purposefully, the plants demonstrate a specific way of communication that is characteristic of the plant world.

When plants talk to each other they speak out of their togetherness, relating to their common matrix, which is guarded and steadily renewed by the devic world. In contrast, human beings are used to speaking out of their isolated selves, which often leads to misunderstandings and conflicts. Ultimately, when whole nations and religions are thinking according to their confined patterns, it can easily lead to unending international conflicts and even to war.

Human beings are certainly different from plants. We should never abolish our individuality. But entering the age when multidimensionality becomes normal, we can think and communicate simultaneously along two paths that seem contradictory. Departing from one's individual matrix allows the possibility of following the way of plants and communicating with the matrix common to all of us that are living, loving, and creating within the earthly universe.

Once again, to emphasize: plants are not meant to substitute for animals in their relation to human evolution. Our relationship to animals, discussed in Part 1, is still relevant. But, under the condition of steady change and to stay attuned to the curves of the Earth Changes, plants can come forward in the name of peace to substitute for animal patterns that patriarchal societies have adopted and misused in the areas of human communication and culture building. To more intensely collaborate with the plant kingdom one needs to gather experiences of the plant essence of the human being. For this, I have included a Gaia Touch hand ritual from *Universe of the Human Body*. This is a gift of a little town in Brazil, Morro do Pilar, that sits upon a sacred hill:

Gaia Touch Hand Ritual
to experience the plant core of the human body

- Position both hands in front of your chest so that one hand is directed upward and the other is horizontal, the palms are touching each other.
- Move the vertical hand upward and the horizontal hand downward. This movement is immediately followed by the opposite one.
- When your hands meet again in front of your chest, make a little pause. Switch the position of the hands, with the palms still touching each other. The previously horizontal position turns into the vertical position, and vice versa.
- Move your hands, as before, one up, the other down, simultaneously.
- Continue with this movement for a while, then finish by imagining that green branches begin growing from your ears.
- How do you feel? Do you experience changes in the quality of your presence?

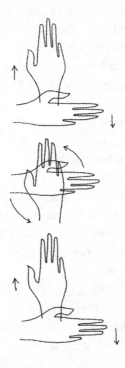

4
Gaia Sparks, sub-elemental worlds, and the all-pervading plasma of life

The year 2018 started with a short but significant dream:

> *I watch a restorer working on an ancient oil painting featuring the dove of the Holy Spirit. He makes a wrong move and breaks through the surface of the painting. The result is a fissure through which I can look into the background of the traditional image of the Holy Spirit. There I see a universe of joyfully dancing light sparks.*

In Christian theology, the Holy Spirit is the third person of the divine Trinity, whose purpose is to bring divine inspiration into the embodied world: to each being, to each social unit, to each cell of each living organism. I believe that I was given a glimpse of the meaning of the Holy Spirit, translated into the ambience of everyday life.

This short dream reminded me of a much longer dream from ten years earlier, during the time I was carving at a Geopuncture stone circle on Fuerteventura, Canaries, together with a group of friends. I previously published that dream in my book *Gaia's Quantum Leap,* but I did not have at that time the clue that came later in the above dream, so my interpretation was not exact then.

> *I am with a group of people at a gas station. We have met occasionally and are speaking in German about the threat of the Earth Changes. At the same time, the daily news is booming from loudspeakers in Slovenian. The two languages clash so unpleasantly that we cannot hear each other.*
>
> *I go to the manager of the gas station to ask him to switch off the loudspeakers. He tells me that this is not so simple, because they do not have an "on/off" switch. He takes me to one of the loudspeakers so that I can see the problem for myself.*

Walking there together with the gas station manager, I realize that I am dealing with an unusual person. With his long white beard, he reminds me more of a spiritual master than a gas station manager.

He says if I will come upstairs with him, then we will surely find the switch. There is in fact a narrow stairway that leads up to the flat roof of the gas station. To my surprise, there is a long wooden cottage, built as if from a fairy tale. The master goes inside to switch the loudspeakers off. I peer through the window and see inside a crowd of small, naked childlike beings who are busily making all sorts of handcrafts that one would not expect from small children.

As I stumble down the steep stairs with the master, the "children" sing a song about the fall of the communist Eastern Block and the fall of the Berlin Wall.

At the same time, I try to remember the names of my dear friends who have already died.

It is obvious that the gas station with its disturbing loudspeakers represents modern civilization, which gets its driving energy from the exploitation of the fossil reserves of the Earth. The manager of the gas station takes on the role of a spiritual master to make clear that his message is coming from the most responsible level of humanity, the so-called spiritual world. The message is that there is no way to solve the immense problems created by the present culture while operating from the same level of existence from which the problems are created. So, it is nonsense to think renewable energy, recycling, reduction in air pollution, etc., can heal our wounded planet.

Instead, he leads the dreamer to another level of reality, symbolized by the fairy cottage on the roof of the gas station, to seek the possibility of a permanent solution. There, the spiritual master presents a specific kind of beings that could help in solving the massive, multiple problems inflicted upon our planet during the thousands of years of patriarchal rule.

The deep-reaching abilities of these beings can be seen in their influence on the surprising fall of the Berlin Wall and the not-at-all expected fall of the communist Soviet empire. But who are these subtle childlike beings, capable of bringing such gigantic changes to completion?

I found the clue in the book of my dear friend William Bloom, *The Christ Sparks,* which I rediscovered in my library after the dream of the restorer working on the image of the Holy Spirit. The book has been in my library since it was published in 1995, but I did not understand its relationship to the present Earth Changes, and I had forgotten about its existence.

The book came into being when William Bloom was unexpectedly contacted by the Sparks in 1987, asking him to write down a message they consider important for humanity at this stage of our evolution. They appeared to him as a large group of beings moving through the atmosphere like a swarm of bees. They are individual beings with their own consciousness dimension and, at the same time, a perfectly interlinked collective. As such, they try to convey to human beings how crucial it is at this time of great changes to develop the sense of a collective or group consciousness. This is not a contradiction to the sense of individuality that modern human beings value above all.

The group of Sparks that contacted William identified itself as accompanying the "Avatar of Synthesis," and hence the name that they choose for themselves, the "Christ Sparks." They identify the Avatar of Synthesis as a highly evolved spirit, originating from the space beyond our galaxy, who has heard the call of the Earth for help in the process of the coming Earth Changes and has touched our planet with his presence and inspiration – the first time in the 1960s. The Sparks accompany him to anchor among humankind (stubbornly continuing along their old paths), his inspiration of a new age of peaceful co-existence among all beings of the Earth.

It is clear from the 2008 dream that the Sparks are not connected exclusively to the Avatar of Synthesis, but are available to help humanity soften the havoc of the approaching Earth Changes. So the question arises as to how to increase our cooperation with the Sparks to match the advancing damages to the Earth and its atmosphere?

Pondering this question I was made aware, through a dream, of severe blockades preventing cooperation between the human family and the Sparks:

I am walking along a corridor and am surprised that all the doors on the left side (leading to the world of the Sparks) are open, while those on the right side are closed.

The ones on the right side represent the blockades. In meditating on the dream, as I approached the doors on both sides, one by one, I felt upon my body the need to identify the blockades and understand their origins. Let me present the result of my examination:

– Where hidden **anger** lies within me at the approaching Earth Changes, pushing me into unknown and unchosen psychic and physical conditions. The Sparks are beings of laughter and joy. The anger vibration blocks them off from humanity.

- Where I experience deep **fear** in facing the intense mixture of destruction and rebuilding necessary with the coming Earth Changes. The Sparks are carriers of bright optimism and an unlimited faith in the wisdom of life. The vibration of fear blocks them off from humanity.
- Where the awareness that the natural and cultural constellations that I love and am used to may get lost or, in best case, substituted with something that I do not know, brings me profound **sorrow**. The Sparks are messengers of beauty and hope. The vibration of sorrow blocks them off from humanity.
- Where, as a human being of the modern age, I feel pushed in a thousand directions by the daily demands of the present hectic way of life, bringing **the loss of concentration and of the ability to be present in the moment**.
- Where human **isolationism** leads to a loss of community and togetherness. This blocks the Sparks from collaboration with the human race. The Sparks' messages to William Bloom are from beings of a perfectly interlinked community. Even though they are spread worldwide, they are aware – in every moment – of the thoughts and feelings of each unit of the swarm. They are spread widely but concentrated to a point.

The list of blockades could certainly be longer. My proposal is to work on transforming these blockades using a method of detachment and transformation at the intercellular level, because we are dealing with blockades that are seated deeply in the subconscious level. This method of transformation is the gift of the Canal Grande in Venice (see p. 73). We also need to better understand the position of the Sparks within the complex earthly universe in order to help build these bridges. Surprisingly, the best model to understand the Sparks' relationship to Gaia and her dragon powers can be found sculpted as a relief on the main portal of the Basilica San Marco in Venice. Although it is nearly a thousand years old, I find it quite accurate. The relief shows Gaia as Mother of Life sitting upon the back of a dragon.

*Gaia upon the dragon from the main portal of the Basilica
San Marco, Venice*

She holds flourishing greenery in her hands that identifies her as the creator of life on Earth. She points to the sphere of dragons as her primary creative tool, with which she can create, decompose, and re-create the manifold Earth cluster of worlds in each moment.

The dimension of the Sparks comes into play at the next stage of creation. They are presented on the relief in the form of a baby dragon growing from the dragon's tail. The baby dragon drinks milk from Gaia's breast. Breastfeeding is life-force, and with it the love and wisdom of the Mother, given to all aspects and beings of life.

According to the model from the Basilica, the Sparks are a community of micro-beings tasked with a wide range of service. They are dedicated to distributing the primeval (sub-atomic) powers, consciousness, and wisdom of Gaia to all beings and levels of her creation. This is why I choose to call them "Gaia Sparks." My insight tells me that the Christ Sparks, about which William Bloom writes, represent a special facet of the Gaia Sparks community with an important task to fulfill in the present age of our planetary evolution.

I asked the Gaia Sparks to propose an exercise through which it would be possible to gather experiences of their presence and to contact them. They proposed the following exercise:

- Sit immersed in inner peace.
- Imagine taking a large step backward.
- Next, simultaneously take a step to the left and to the right, forming two figures of yourself behind your back.
- Both figures should simultaneously take a large step forward. Now three of you are standing in a row.
- The left and right figures simultaneously step toward the "you" at the center. Now you are one again.
- A square-like space behind your back has been created. This is the place of your possible communion with the Gaia Sparks. Do not turn around to look at them. Rather, invite them closer into your heart space. It helps if you imagine yourself as a small child. The Gaia Sparks are in harmony with little children.

- If the exercise is not successful for you, consider working on detachment concerning the above aspects of blockage toward the Gaia Sparks (pp. 117-118) before attempting the exercise again.

In recent years the Gaia Sparks have attracted human attention through the appearance of colorful little spheres called "Orbs." They usually appear on photographs taken at some important locations or in connection with events that have a special energy. Outwardly they look like tiny spheres, but seen from within, they are intelligent beings, the Sparks. Gaia Sparks have decided to show themselves to offer human beings their cooperation with the intent to accelerate personal or planetary processes of change.

Since the Gaia Sparks seem to be of great importance in the process of Earth Changes, is it possible to take them up on their offer of collaborating with them? I am myself exploring the possibility of collaboration using my own chakras from the feminine chakra system of the five Elements (see p. 87).

Two of those chakras are focused on the soles of the feet and two on the palms of the hands. These belong to the chakras of the Air element. They are identified in Christian tradition as "stigmata Christi."

Their background myth connects them to the wounds inflicted upon the Christ body during the crucifixion.

Besides these four, there is a fifth stigmata, which is positioned on the right side of the thorax, at the level of the pointed breastbone's end. Its origin is connected with the spear of the soldier Longinus, who pierced the thorax of the Christ to make sure that he was dead. This center is also part of the composition of the feminine chakras of the five elements. It is in resonance with the element Water.

Leaving behind the mythological origin of the five chakras, they can be recognized as interdimensional portals through which the Sparks can enter into the manifested world to perform a specific task supporting Gaia's creative processes. Human beings can act as a bridge along which the Sparks can enter the manifested world to accelerate a specific process of change and transformation.

Why would our role as mediator be important in this case? It is important because we have the capacity to connect the cosmic impulse of the Christ Sparks with the earthly quality of the Gaia Sparks.

What is the purpose of the synthesis that comes into being if the cosmic and the earthly aspects of the Sparks merge? It is not just a synthesis of earthly and cosmic consciousness but also a connection between the elements of Air (hand/feet chakras) and Water (fifth stigmata). The synthesis of Air and Water elements is of decisive importance in building the new space of reality that should replace the old Earth of the Earth element.

What is the purpose of the synthesis of the elements Air and Water? The Air element, that is, the element of consciousness, is too lofty on its own to offer space to the evolutions that explore matter in its various facets. This is why the element Water is needed to serve as a medium of embodiment. Water is capable of storing all the information needed for the new space of reality to appear as a relatively solid ambience but be fluid and open to all the parallel worlds.

Finally, what appearance will the Sparks take in passing through the five portals? They appear like colorful air bubbles dispersing from the mouth of a person immersed in water.

Now we are ready for an exercise to initiate collaboration with the Sparks in order to support the work of Gaia to create the new space of reality:

- Be aware of your belly cavity as the sphere containing Gaia's primeval (dragon) powers. Feel its quality being in resonance with the divine core of the planet.
- Be aware of the sphere of your heart system contained within the space of your thorax. Feel its quality connected to the cosmic source, named above as the Avatar of Synthesis.
- Imagine that the two spheres merge within your body, and are centered now in your elemental heart, at the level of your lowest breastbone.
- Imagine that the sphere is being broken down, step by step, into countless microspheres identical with the Sparks. They are similar to colorful air bubbles.
- Then release the Sparks in the form of a continuous chain of air bubbles through your fifth stigmata-chakra into the environment. Help yourself by breathing deeply.
- Now the four stigmata-chakras in your hands and feet come into play. Your hands are open, your feet upon the ground. The subtle information issuing from them, perhaps in the form of colored rays, transmits the matrix of the new space of reality that the Sparks are about to build.
- Imagine yourself within the sphere of the new space and be aware of its qualities. Enlarge the sphere so that it encompasses your home and finally also the Earth as a whole. Give thanks while the process of releasing the Sparks is continuing.

The fifth stigmata, being a chakra of the Water element, can also serve as an interdimensional portal through which the Gaia Sparks enter into the inner spaces of the human body to work on regenerating and healing. Use the following conscious four-sequence breathing process for this purpose:

- While breathing in, invite the Gaia Sparks to enter your body through the fifth-stigmata interdimensional portal. (This portal prevents rubbish from entering your body.)
- While breathing out, lead the Sparks through the organs of your body, specifically where their service is needed.
- Using the next inhale, lead the Sparks back to the portal of the fifth stigmata to be released from your body.
- Through the following exhale, release the Sparks so that they can return to the environment. Then start again with the next inhale.

Besides the subtle levels of existence, it is important to also mention their corresponding expression in the organism of manifested life. The dragon power, for example, manifests as atomic power. The matrices of different life forms manifest as genetic codes. In this sense, one can consider the almost infinite community of microbes as the manifested forms of the Gaia Sparks.

The global community of microbes represents the aspect of the Sparks that reaches into the materialized world. Microbes, constituting different levels and facets of the plasma of life, are considered the oldest living beings upon the Earth, several billions of years old. Scientists have discovered that they are highly intelligent and life supporting. It is said that a cubic meter of healthy soil contains more microbes than there are human beings upon the planet. There are about four pounds of these infinitely small life forms present within each human being. Of course they are everywhere in our environment, in constant movement and exchange between the worlds inside and outside. Without this so-called "microbiome," life upon the embodied level of the Earth would not be possible.

5
The Universal Goddess in her new role as Indigo Gaia

When speaking of Gaia as an Earth Goddess, she should not be imagined as something static, as a sculpture upon the altar of eternity or an immense light shining out of the center of Earth's cluster of worlds. On the contrary, Gaia moves with her creation, transforming herself from one sequence of evolution to another. One can expect that in the present Earth transmutation process Gaia is also about to change her identity.

In the beginning, she was known to the human race as the Mother of Life. Her image was presented carved in Paleolithic cave dwellings and as clay figurines such as the famous Venus of Willendorf. At the threshold of the Neolithic age, when agriculture and social life were invented, the all-embracing Gaia transformed into a triple goddess representing the cycle of life. Let me characterize her three phases briefly:

- White Goddess (spring): wholeness connecting Heaven and Earth;
- Red Goddess (high summer): abundance and the interaction between the feminine and masculine principles;
- Black Goddess (late autumn and winter): transformation, death, and regeneration.

During the following patriarchal age, Gaia had to hide within various symbolic figures of the feminine deities, adapting to the will of the new polytheistic or monotheistic religions. In Christianity, for example, her triple constitution appears hidden behind the figure of Mary, the mother of Jesus of Nazareth. She became venerated as the Virgin Mary (white aspect), the Mother of God Madonna (red aspect) and the Black Madonna (black aspect).

This brief overview of the past is needed in order to relate to the present transformation of Gaia. But be aware that the past is inherent within the present, and also the future.

Gaia showed to me her changes related to the present Earth trans-muting process in a vivid dream in 2002 in Madrid, a dream in which she herself was present with all her strength and beauty:

At first, to identify herself, Gaia appears as a giant, well propor-tioned, dark-skinned woman dancing about from place to place. Every muscle of her body is moving in wavelike fashion, accompa-nied by the roaring of a thousand oceans. She then starts to show me the ongoing transformations of her presence.

— *I realize that, at certain moments, her magnificent female body is temporarily assuming masculine features—appearing as a male. Gaia states that she does not support the feminine-masculine (yin-yang) opposition. The figure of God becomes integrated within the Goddess. The assumption that the period dominated by God would be followed by a Goddess-dominated age is shown as nonsense. Instead, we approach an age of partnership between the feminine and masculine principles.*

— *My attention is now on Gaia's left hand where she holds something like an apple, as some ancient goddesses are depicted. Looking closer I realize that "the apple" is composed of two childlike figures sticking together in the form of an apple. One is innocent and happy, the other burdened with a heavy cross. I interpret the symbol as a promise of the new Gaia to create a synthesis between Eastern spirituality as initiated by Buddha and Western spirituality as inspired by the Christ. Buddha can be seen as the avatar of spiritual freedom and the Christ as teaching humanity how to meet the challenges of ordinary life. When connected, they represent the foundation of a new "trans-religious" spirituality.*

— *Next, my attention is led to Gaia's face. I see it in the process of a surprising change. At first her facial features show the uplifted cosmic quality often seen in the goddess images of some ancient cultures. In the second phase, Gaia's facial features become ever more human. Looking with awe at her changing face, I understand that she is leaving behind her status as divinity to become a*

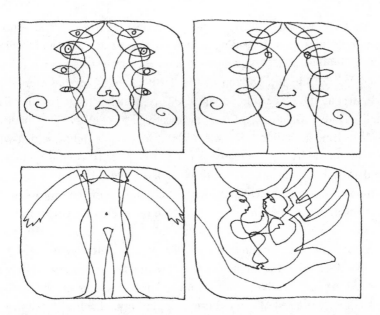

*partner of humanity and others in her evolutions. As mentioned,
this was made clear through the quality of the whole dream.
She herself is present here and now, no more speaking from the
distant center of the earthly universe.*

— *Then Gaia shows her intentions for helping humanity, while meeting the more and more difficult challenges of the Earth Changes.
I suddenly notice a drastic change of direction of the waves undu-
lating upon the surface of her thighs. As a consequence of the
contradicting directions of the waves two peaceful strips or islands
are formed there, untouched by the roaring sea.*

My recent interpretation of the image of the islands is that it is Gaia's
promise to human beings that when they are tuned to the creative and
life-supporting aspects of the Earth Changes, islands of (relative) peace
will be provided for shelter and protection to use as the bases from which
to enter situations of turmoil and offer help to those caught unprepared
by the tsunami of change. Outwardly they do not need to show a difference from other environments because their peace and stability is
anchored upon another level of existence, a causal one.

Another inspiring transformation of Gaia concerns her red aspect, the one dedicated to spreading abundance upon the planet and feeding all the innumerable beings moving upon the Earth – the human family included. Within the horizon of the Earth Changes she has started to manifest another face of her divine presence, which is related to the color indigo. Indigo Gaia represents a new creative aspect of the Red Goddess.

Appearing as Indigo Gaia, she is about to set up conditions that will enable humanity to co-create what we need to survive and be happy and to uphold our culture with all of its range of activities. Plants, animals, stones and elemental beings will be part of the process, each one fulfilling its role within this new kind of co-creative community of embodied beings.

Speaking practically, Indigo Gaia is revealing a new geomantic system in the landscape, a network of consciousness combining different aspects of the creative process into a kind of spatial necklace. The system is composed of intersecting spindle forms. Each of these forms represents different qualities needed in the process of creating. The elements that come into being through the intersection of the spindle forms stand for interdimensional portals that make possible the transition from one field into another. This is independent from the islands of peace, and there certainly might be other ones.

This new landscape system transforms the Earth itself into an intelligent co-creative being, which at the same time is a source of learning and re-connecting with the wisdom of the earthly universe and its beings. The body of the landscape and cityscape is about to become identical with the body and consciousness of Indigo Gaia. This means that in the near future (partly already now) gardening or sculpting a stone will have the equivalence of studying a book of holy wisdom or praying to the divine presence for creating the conditions for a fulfilled life.

To help connect with the geomantic system of Indigo Gaia, I offer a Gaia Touch personal ritual that is a gift of the cityscape of the Slovenian town Celje, where I gathered my first experiences of the spindle form system. The gestures together create the spindle form and lead the exercise to an opening of the heart.

Gaia Touch Personal Ritual to connect with the creative network of Indigo Gaia

- Start with both hands crossing above your coccyx to mark the lower corner of the spindle form and connect with the primeval powers of Gaia.

- Lift your hands above your head and hold them crossed there to mark the upper corner of the spindle form and to connect with the cosmic wisdom called Sophia.

- After you have marked the lower and the upper corners of the spindle, mark the two side ones. Start with your hands open, as the drawing on the following page shows.

- Put the left hand upon the right side of your chest, while the right hand stays on its place.

- This gesture is followed by the same open gesture again.

- After a short pause put the right hand upon the left side of your chest, while the left one stays on its place.

- Then both hands show the open gesture again.

- After a short pause put both hands upon your chest so that they cross each other in front of your heart center.

- Then open both hands widely to share the quality of Indigo Gaia with your environment and the world.

- After repeating the ritual a few times, stay for a while with your eyes closed to examine what Gaia's presence might want to tell you at this moment.

This ritual is in resonance with the creative system of Indigo Gaia and also exists within the micro-landscape of the human body. In the case of the human being, the creative system is composed of three spindle forms that intersect two times.

All together there are five spindle forms, representing the five phases of the creative process. The following interpretation presents a route that any creative process can adopt if the creating person is in tune with the new space of reality that comes into being through the transformation of the Red Goddess into Indigo Gaia. In effect, here we are dealing with the new causal background of any creative process.

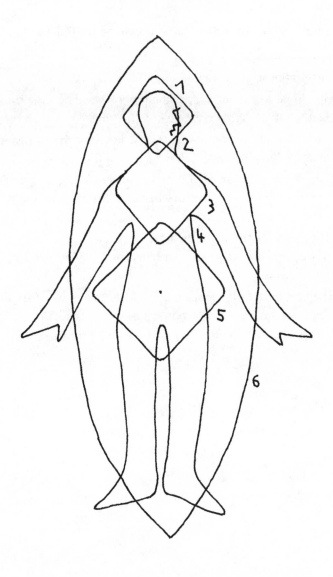

The creative system of Indigo Gaia in the human body

The interpretation of the five phases could be the following:

1. The space of the head as the melting pot of creative ideas and inspirations.
2. The throat as an interdimensional portal enabling the transformation of ideas into creative imaginations.
3. The space of the multidimensional heart system infusing the creative imaginations with the spark of life.
4. The elemental heart as an interdimensional portal, transforming imaginations so that they become blueprints for the embodiment of the given process.
5. The space of the belly as a treasury of the primeval dragon powers, making possible that blueprints can become embodied phenomena.
6. The mandorla form embracing the body makes us aware that at the final stage a bodily action is needed to secure that the given phenomenon becomes living and breathing reality.

6
Counterforces working secretly to undermine the upcoming age of peace

Do not naively think that the transmutation process of the Earth and humanity will run smoothly, because there are powerful counterforces that are working to keep the old models of existence functioning, even though the old models are obviously in a state of decay.

The situation in which we find ourselves is not a simple one to grasp, nor is there a simple solution. Although more and more people are becoming aware and realizing that they do not want to live in a consumer-driven society whose other face is a state of being involved in continual wars, they are being held prisoners (usually unknowingly) by powers that hide the fact that Gaia offers a clear and practical alternative.

A recent dream of mine gives a realistic insight into the mechanics of the work of the counterforces:

I am driving with some friends in a car. Ahead there is an unusual vehicle that we want to pass. It has four-wheels and is carrying a large traditional container for transporting manure. It has no driver and no motor, and yet it is moving with crazy speed, at least 100 miles per hour. The road in front of us is absolutely straight, leading toward a zero point. I am worried. To follow our intended path, we must make a left turn up ahead. We need to pass the manure truck before making the turn, but we are following three cars driving parallel to each other that prevent our passing. The drivers are obviously talking to each other through the open windows. We will soon arrive at the required turn, but the three cars in front are blocking our view. At the speed we are traveling, the important turn could easily be missed.

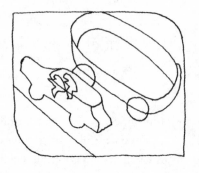

The image in the first part of the dream is clearly about the connection between the development of modern high technology and the resulting pollution of the planetary environment – the self-driving truck with a full load of manure.

Many individuals and groups that are not ready to live in such schizophrenic conditions are looking for alternatives. Their wish is the possible turn to the left away from the "road to hopelessness." The message of the dream then comes forward. There are powers and groups within society that consciously obstruct the fulfillment of global and individual transformation. The drivers of the three cars who are talking to each other at the critical turning point represent counterforces secretly working to undermine the upcoming age of peace.

Practically, this is being done in many different ways, for example by hiding information from the public awareness that although the ongoing "climate changes" are threatening the life of the planet, they are also opening a new and highly valuable prospective for the further evolution of the human being, our culture, and all other beings of Gaia's universe.

To summarize, there are three levels upon which the obstruction against the process of change works:

1. People of the Earth are afraid of the essential Earth Changes knocking at the door of their psyche. They are puzzled about the challenges that the Earth Changes are bringing with them, while immersed in their existential worries and the hectic consumerism

that the counterforces consciously infiltrate into modern society. As a result, dark clouds of negatively charged powers build up in the etheric atmosphere, hindering the smooth flow of the incoming Earth Changes.

2. There are political, religious, and other types of groups and networks that selfishly want the present reality unchanged in order to protect their social and economic status. As conditions deteriorate, they require ever more sophisticated measures to keep the old space of reality functional. They ignore the calls for change and consciously persist in obstructionist activities toward individuals and groups that support the ongoing Earth transmuting process.

3. A third kind of obstructing presence, the most difficult to recognize, and which is interfering on a global scale, is known by many names: "Devil," "Lucifer," "Anti-Christ," etc. This is the "Cosmic Challenger," leading humanity in the wrong direction, trapping us in an extremely limited time and space condition.

Be aware that whatever happens can be redeemed if we can discover its positive aspect. From this point of view, the work of the Cosmic Challenger can be seen as a means to awaken the human psyche and consciousness, to recognize and detach from the alienated state in which humanity is now lost. His activity upon the Earth can be understood as an expression of cosmic wisdom that contains the knowledge to awaken human beings using intrigue and dramatic upheavals to snap us out of our complacency and back on a rightful path.

Finally, I want to emphasize that there exists another effective pattern used by the counterforces. It is a perverted form of the Christian pattern of the Last Judgment. This unhappy pattern is an invention of those individuals and institutions that do not trust the divine guidance of the human race. Instead, they infiltrate into the collective memory the pattern of an inevitable division between "Good" and "Bad."

Seen in the context of the ongoing Earth Changes, the "good people" will be those who are obedient and follow the mass patterns of behavior or religious rules, or are simply asleep. For them, a world sphere is being prepared step by step where life loses any natural quality, becoming fully digitalized. Their focused attachment to the material world and their feeling of safety that comes from following the masses can cause their loss of freedom and creative potential to pass unnoticed.

Those interested in truthful and loving relationships among themselves and with other beings of Gaia's universe – the less numerous part of humanity – are being identified as the "bad people," slapped with the humiliating name "New Agers," and told to just disappear.

This is a dangerous pattern that needs to be consciously transmuted. It is true that humanity seems totally fragmented at this time of Change as if there would be no common matrix connecting us. But this is not the reality. What is real is the common matrix that connects not only us embodied people, but includes also those abiding in the spiritual world of the ancestors and descendants. Not one single individual, no matter how distorted she or he appears inside world affairs, is excluded. The extreme diversity of paths we are walking is useful because together we can gather all the experiences needed so that we can become a race of autonomous and yet connected beings, co-creators of the Earth cluster of worlds and beyond – never again followers of any kind of illusion.

Exercises of detachment might help in situations where you are under pressure from the first two of the opposing forces. The Gaia Touch hand ritual of detachment that I presented previously (Bali version, p. 50) can help you liberate yourself from false ideas or energy patterns.

In more severe cases, the following hand ritual of detachment can help:

Gaia Touch Hand Ritual of detachment – No. 2

- Hold your hands horizontally in front of your solar plexus, squeeze them powerfully together. Have the purpose of your detachment in your mind.
- Then pull your hands apart with optimum power to annihilate the given attachment.

If you are in conflict with the second and the third counterforces, then my council is to first look inside yourself for an unrecognized weakness that makes you susceptible to their arrows. A trauma, blockage, or false intent within an individual or a group creates a resonance bridge that can be used by the counterforces to control behavior. There is no way to hold back the attack of the counterforces in this situation. They can use the principle of the resonance bridge to successfully connect to the cause inside the individual, whether the person wants it or not.

There are two Gaia Touch exercises to build a protective aura. In both cases the sacred geometrical form of the mandorla is implemented. The exercise with the whole body involved can be found in my book *Universe of the Human Body.* Here is its form translated into hand movements that can be done quickly and discretely when you are in a public place:

Gaia Touch Hand Ritual of protection with the help of the mandorla form

- To portray the two points of the mandorla form, use the base of the hand for one side and the tip of the middle finger for the other.
- The protective mandorla is drawn three times diagonally in the upward direction and three times in the downward direction, moving the hands back and forth as described.
- While drawing the mandorla have the feeling that you stand inside the created structure, which finally is of a spherical nature.

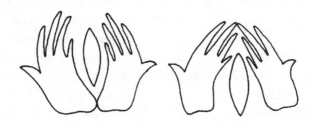

7
How to be creative in the conditions of dramatic changes

If the basic constitution of the manifested world is changing we will need some new tools to continue being creative under these new conditions. Be aware that the future and the past are mental concepts, and that we need new tools for creating optimal conditions for our existence now. The following dream in 2015 made me aware of this need:

I am riding in a fancy white bus on a wide road that is overloaded with traffic. The situation is making the driver crazy. He abandons the bus in the middle of the road and disappears.

None of the travelers has the courage to take the steering wheel. So I do. The problem is that never in my life have I ever learned how to drive (This is actually true!)

Surprisingly, it goes quite well. But then we arrive at the top of a steep slope. The problem is that I cannot find the brake!

Fortunately, I notice that at the left side of the steering wheel there is a rounded membrane. The closer I get with my left hand to the membrane, the slower the bus descends, and vice versa. I also have the feeling that by embracing the forefront of the bus with my right hand, I can prevent it physically from rushing down the road.

Along the steep slope, the road is no longer paved. It looks like a plowed field. It seems that we are the first ones to use it as a road.

At the half-way point down the slope I stop the bus, with the help of the membrane, because I have started to doubt its effectiveness. Turning around to the travelers, I ask if somebody can explain the mechanics of traditional brakes.

I get some senseless answers from a few people. And some others show me complicated technical schemes that I don't understand at all.

I contemplate pushing stones under the wheels to secure it in place and going out to find my wife, who is an excellent driver.

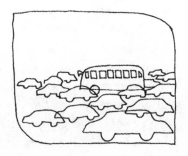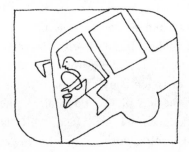

One of the keys to understanding the message of the dream is the change of the road into freshly plowed ground on transitioning from level ground to the steep slope. Both symbols, the change in direction and the loss of the road, warn of the beginning of a more dramatic chapter of Earth Changes. The dream suggests that we stay creative in our situation, and not be broken by the appearance of the new, more difficult circumstances that are presently manifesting.

The principle underlying the new technology seems to be a crazy one. Even though the dreamer is actually able to stop the bus on the steep slope through use of the membrane, he still doubts the ability of the membrane to stop the bus!

At this point the dream is very clear that doubt blocks the new technology, making it useless. So what is the source of power for the new technology if doubt can destroy it? It is obviously a technology based upon the capacities of consciousness.

At this point, it is useful to note that "technology," as it is translated from ancient Greek, is "the manner by which a thing is gained." The modern idea that technology must be connected to something mechanistic limits by our use of that word.

Consciousness, by itself, is too ethereal to actually manage and move situations in the embodied world. But the dream points to a specific aspect of consciousness called "imagination." Imagination is the creative aspect of consciousness and works through the creation of inner images. Beware: this imagination is not identical to visualization, which operates at the mental level. This imagination works on the synergy of combining information arriving from the causal (archetypal, cosmic) treasury with the creative intent of the creator. The membrane at the left side of the steering wheel together with the dreamer's desire to hold the bus back with his right hand is an accurate symbol for this.

As an example of this kind of technology from my experience: the Gaia Touch body and hand rituals that we have used while traveling in the bus of this book along the road and non-road of the Earth Changes. As I mentioned, the Gaia Touch personal and group rituals are inspired during group-based geomantic or Earth healing work with specific places or landscapes. This means that the technology of Gaia Touch exercises is the result of the interaction between a group of people dedicated to Gaia and the health of her universe, on the one hand, and on the other, the human capacity to translate inspiration into images and then furthermore into body movements.

For example, I get a general notion of how the movement should look. I then need to design it so that it runs smoothly and so that its sequences can be communicated to other people.

When you are performing the Gaia Touch movements, the link with the elemental beings and the specific qualities of the place of its origin are being activated. Connection is possible because of the existing resonance between your movements and the source of their origin. The source does not always need to be connected to a place. Often it is linked with a specific spiritual source and the beings embodying it.

During the first decade of their use I called those exercises "holographic touch" to make clear that is a kind of ultra soft technology based upon the principle of a hologram.

It is also important to mention that Gaia Touch is an open system that everybody is free to use if their intent is lovingly connected with the aim of personal inner development and the will to support the transmutation processes of Gaia, which will lead to a new age of peace and creative co-existence among all beings of her universe. The system also allows for the further evolution of some of the exercises, teaching them to others and creating new ones according to the principles described.

Another example of "consciousness technology" that I use is the "cosmogram," which is carved in stone or wood, or executed in bronze or glass, or simply as drawings. They represent visual signs in which a multidimensional message is encoded. Cosmograms carrying multidimensional content are not conveying a logical message like modern signs created for practical or symbolic purposes. Cosmograms carry a message encoded at numerous levels simultaneously. At one level they can be perceived as energetic patterns, from another point of view as codifications of cosmic archetypes, and at yet another level as visual signs.

Consequently, cosmograms can serve as a means of communication for contacting other conscious beings or moving certain processes at different levels of existence:

- They can be used as a medium to contact spiritual or elemental beings that are not able to perceive messages in a physical form.
- They can be implemented to move energies and create communication bridges on the invisible levels.
- As visible forms, they are useful for conveying messages to the logical mind, which perceives exclusively at the physical level.
- They can also be carriers of soul presence, serving as a possibility for certain spiritual qualities or beings to become embodied here and now.

To be able to serve as pluridimensional signs, cosmograms should be created as a synthesis of logical and intuitive creative processes. Working on the aesthetic level is supplemented with artistic inspiration that comes into being through a heart to heart communication with the place for which the given cosmogram is being created.

Cosmograms have a peculiarity that distinguishes them from all other kinds of symbols. They must be created in such a way that they are not just objective forms, but they are imbued with their own quality of energy and their own consciousness. On one side, they address the viewer at a personal level, on the other, they are capable of relatively autonomous activity within the given environment. They work on the basis of mutual exchange between the partners involved in communication and not merely as transmitters of information as with ordinary symbols.

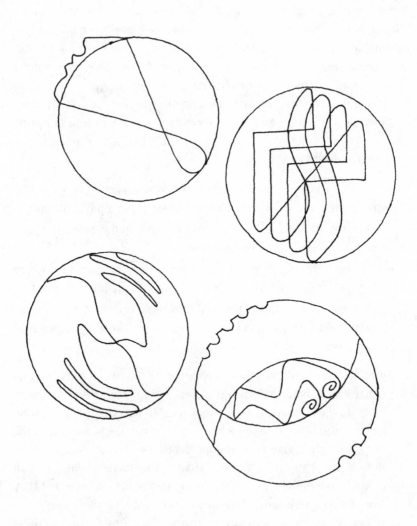

Cosmograms carved for geopuncture projects

8

Transformation of matter – the world appearing as a hologram

Speaking about changes to physical reality brings up a dangerous matter: the feeling of a loss of orientation and of losing one's way in an unknown space. It might feel more comfortable to remain ignorant. Yet it is better to be ready for the changes appearing at the embodied level that we share with stones, animals, plants, and landscapes than to become overwhelmed by unknown situations.

In 2017, I received a deeply encoded dream that may help us to understand what is going on at the highly sensitive level of the human psyche:

I am sitting next to the window in a train with Hanna, the editor of my early books on the subject of Earth Changes and human destiny. The train passes a huge industrial block-like building made of concrete. I notice that the building is not in good shape. There are cracks on its walls and in some parts of its grounds.

When we arrive at the station, we begin walking on our path. Unexpectedly, we find ourselves standing in front of a wonderful tall stone structure. Looking at the gigantic megalith, I am so excited that I nearly forget to breathe. It is as high as a skyscraper and of a marvelous natural form, colored in vivid brown shades.

I wish to explore the megalith's geomantic dimensions. But after trying different approaches, I have to admit that there is no way to come close to the high stone because it is surrounded by private homes, with private gardens and private paths that lead to their own doors.

Hannah is speaking with a man who is dressed completely in white, who has casually appeared with a big white dog close to the megalith. After speaking with the man, she approaches me with the information that the megalith is not called "Baldur," but "Valdur."

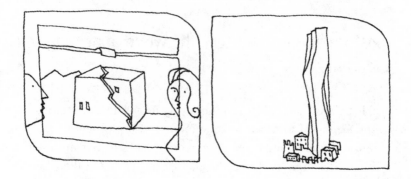

Working with the dream when it first appeared in my consciousness, I believed that the obvious contradiction between the decaying concrete building and the powerful megalith would represent the proper key to arrive at the dream's message. My conclusion then was that we are leaving the old cultural structures behind as we move toward being embraced by Gaia and her powerful nature.

Unfortunately, this was a misleading conclusion. Rather, I assert now that the boxy industrial building and the gigantic phallic megalith are both equally problematic. They represent two faces of a civilization that has lost the right to continue its evolution upon the planet.

In effect, the fascination of the dreamer in front of the megalith soon dissolved with the realization that the majestic stone is a prisoner of the egocentric human families settled at its base.

The change of the megalith's name from Baldur to Valdur hints that there was a manipulation done upon its matrix so that its original purpose was twisted. In the Slovenian language, the letters "V" and "B" can be easily exchanged without noticing the difference – this happens often. But the man in white with his white dog stands witness that this change was made purposefully, and probably within an occult context.

The Valdur dream is clear about the present condition of material reality being manipulated. What we experience today as matter is not what Gaia intended. With the help of the elemental beings of the four elements, consciousness was tightly condensed, bringing the embodied world sphere into existence. As a result, an evolution such as humankind's evolution could get valuable experiences that the conditions of more subtle worlds, such as the etheric ones, do not permit. Living for a limited time in the materialized world, people can attain direct experience of the effects on reality that their intentions, for good or for bad, trigger. Such experiences accelerate their spiritual growth immensely.

The Valdur dream also brings awareness that the original intent of Gaia has been changed by the will power of human beings incarnating age after age into the sphere of materialized reality. Using the capacities of rational logic, coupled with the patriarchal ideology that considers feminine qualities as inferior, the sphere of matter has been over-condensed. The resulting density of matter prevents the free exchange between the manifested world and its precious causal sources.

I must admit that, at this point, I can clearly perceive the influence of the Cosmic Challenger, whose intent might be to cut humanity off from its spiritual roots, and by this, to enslave the human race within a confined, over-materialized space broken off from the divine intent of Gaia and from the intention of the spiritual world to lead humanity to becoming free creators of their own destiny.

Three indicators of the Challenger's plan appeared in the dream:

— The broken and deserted industrial building presents the modern human world as alienated and not capable of securing the future evolution of human culture.

— The oversized, phallic megalith attests to the dominance that male power asserts over the human psyche and civilization.

— The humans settled at the base of the megalith are characterized by their selfish and introverted attitude, ignorant of the power of life that vibrates at the back of the settlement.

Another dream from a few years ago may inspire a way to overcome the threatening dominance of the one-sided male principle and enable human beings to again enjoy the beauty of the material world unencumbered by the hidden trap of over-materialization:

A sort of a funny-looking elemental master takes me in his car to show me an important place. I know that he is an elemental master because his car drives with the two right wheels upon the earthly road and with the other two upon the air beside the road.

He shows me a gigantic canyon, in effect, a channel cut into stone walls. He wants to make me aware that in the channel there is a river of tremendous potential inherent in human beings but totally forgotten, dried out, and even blocked. This river of primeval power should flow into everyday life, adding enormous enhancement to life's quality and vitality.

Pondering the above dream, I discovered that there are three such horizontal power channels within the human multidimensional body. If activated they could perfectly balance the oversized vertical channel represented in the previous dream by the Valdur megalith. The masculine vertical flow, connecting the core of the Earth with the center of our galaxy, should be balanced with three horizontal channels linking the archetypal/causal dimensions behind our back with the manifested/embodied life in front. Their horizontal nature identifies them as a powerful feminine (yin) quality. These three Gaia power channels run on three levels of our body:

— The first channel runs through the center of the belly region, bringing primeval (dragon) powers into our manifested life to give us, as human beings, strength in our willingness to support Gaia in her endeavors to recreate the Earth as a place of peace and beauty.

— The second horizontal power channel connects the cosmic back region of the heart system with the front heart region – dedicated to the expansion of love and compassion into the world around us.

— The "third eye" channel links the wisdom of the individual soul, pulsating at the back of the head, with the knowledge needed for an individual to create her or his life as a valuable time of learning, of walking the paths of fulfilled existence and enjoying the beauty of life.

I offer the following breathing exercise to activate the three feminine horizontal power fields, and by this to balance the exaggerated masculine dominance. It has three sequences, and in the name of balance also includes the masculine vertical channel:

The First Sequence, for the area of the belly:

- Start by inhaling from the core of the Earth, leading your breath upward until the point behind the navel is reached.
- Exhale from that point, simultaneously and horizontally in all directions, so that a power field of feminine quality comes into being.
- Inhale from all directions of the field simultaneously and breathe out into the universe. Take a short pause.
- Now inhale from the center of the universe and lead your breath down until the point behind the navel is reached.
- Exhale simultaneously and horizontally in all directions.
- Finally, inhale from all directions of the horizontal field simultaneously and exhale into the core of the Earth. Take a short pause, and then repeat this pattern of breathing several times.

The Second sequence, for the area of the heart:

- Start by inhaling from the core of the Earth, leading your breath upward until the point of the heart center is reached.
- Exhale out from the heart center simultaneously and horizontally in all directions, so that a power field of feminine quality comes into being.
- Inhale from all directions of the field simultaneously and breathe out into the universe. Take a short pause.
- Now inhale from the center of the universe and lead your breath down until the heart center is reached.
- Exhale simultaneously and horizontally in all directions.
- Finally, inhale from all directions of the horizontal field of the heart simultaneously and exhale into the core of the Earth. Take a short pause, and then repeat this pattern of breathing several times.

The Third Sequence, for the area of the third eye:

- Start by inhaling from the core of the Earth, leading your breath upward until the point of the third eye is reached. Be aware that the third eye pulsates at the center of the skull cavity, behind the symbolic point above the eye brows.
- Exhale out from the center of the third eye simultaneously and horizontally in all directions, so that a power field of feminine quality comes into being.
- Inhale from all directions of the field simultaneously and breathe out into the universe. Take a short pause.
- Now inhale from the center of the universe and lead your breath down till the point of the third eye is reached.
- Exhale simultaneously and horizontally in all directions.
- Finally, inhale from all directions of the horizontal field of the third eye simultaneously and then exhale into the core of the Earth. Take a short pause, and then repeat this pattern of inhaling and exhaling several times.

It is alright if during the exercise the yin channels dissolve into horizontal energy fields or even into spheres. This is nothing more than different phases of their existence.

On the morning after I did the above breathing ritual, something unexpected happened. In a vision, the Valdur megalith exploded and in the same instant the shining presence of Gaia as the White Goddess appeared in its place.

This vision can be interpreted in the following way: If the dense structure of the material world could be balanced with the horizontal powers/feminine qualities, then it could become the basis of a new transparent and yet material body of reality. This transparent and material reality could be perceived by beings that have no physical eyes.

As a consequence, this new quality of matter coming into being through the Earth's changing process would not hinder communication between the different spheres of the Earth cluster; instead, it would make communication possible between them, and it would become normal for beings who are embodied in the new material world to perceive the subtle realities that until now were excluded from their perception. A new age of collaboration with our invisible allies would be opened.

9
Plan "A" to avoid cataclysms

In recent reports about the Earth Changes, the idea of an Earth pole shift is often mentioned. This does not mean that the globe will turn around physically, rather the energetic charge of the poles would be exchanged, probably causing unprecedented effects for the living beings upon the planet as well as for its vital fields. Indeed, changes are inevitable upon a planet that is on the way to another epoch of its evolution. However, the idea of a pole reversal does not take into consideration the love of Gaia toward her creation, which I know from my many experiences.

I had a dream in late autumn 2018 that explains why a kind of reset of the life systems might be inevitable.

I look into the back of a car and see a large open backpack. The feeling is as if the back of my head would be open. Looking inside I see a mechanism that I recognize as a classical gramophone. There are seven to eight black discs positioned one above the other. The mechanism is designed for a single disc to fall down for the music coded on that disc to play. After the music is finished on that disc, the next is dropped, and then the next one.... But in this case I am surprised to see that the upper disc is ready to play its music, not the lowest one.

The dreamer understands now that the lower discs represent the music that has already played, that is, they represent the past epochs in the Earth's evolution. At this point in time a new disc should enter the mechanism to play its music. From the analysis in the first part of the book, this music is in resonance with the Air element.

At this point something strange happens in the dream. The set of discs becomes pancakes that are positioned neatly one above the other. The dreamer understands that the pile of discs has been exchanged with a pile of pancakes because the discs, representing the matrix of an age, do not carry just technical information but the codes of life itself.

> *Yet, looking at the upper pancake, poised to enter the mechanism to be played, upsets me. The upper pancake is thick and swollen. It does not fit into the fine mechanism that would enable it to play its music. Without success, I try to help by pushing the pancake into the opening of the mechanism with my hand. Finally I give up, saying to myself: "A solution could be to take the whole pack of discs out and do a kind of reset."*

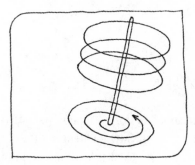 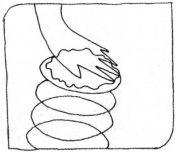

This dream does not say anything about how the reset of Gaia's life systems could happen nor how we as human beings embodied within Gaia's life systems should react or behave. Some seers speak about three days and nights of darkness during which we should stay inside and not even stick our nose out of our house. The following recent dream might give more information about the predicted reset.

> *I am walking over a wide flat landscape with one of my assistants. Suddenly the landscape starts to lift up on one side, reaching about an 80 degree inclination. With great effort, we continue to walk along the now almost vertical plane, believing the upper edge of the plane to be the only place to stand balanced as we are used to in our former spatial condition.*
>
> *My assistant succeeds in reaching the thin edge of the vertical plane. She discovers that she can stand perfectly and in balance,*

even though the edge is so narrow as to not allow enough space for the complete soles of her feet. She even offers a helping hand to me, when I am unable to walk the last five or six feet. I am exhausted but, surprisingly, refuse any help. Instead, I warn her not to fall down from her precarious perch. What saves me from falling into the abyss is a foothold on a small dead bush.

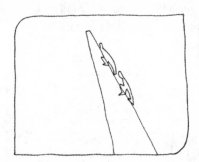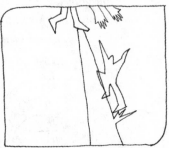

The dream confirms that a reset could be an inevitable part of the future Earth Changes. It also gives a hint of how challenging the situation will be for human beings that are attached to certain conditions of gravity and would be lost if the conditions change drastically. What would be left of the old space – as in the dream – would be a thin edge, too narrow for a human being to stand upon.

The dream also delivers information that might be useful in the case of a reset like the pole reversal. It indicates that the effort to hang on to the old conditions of gravity in the new spatial circumstances will be useless. Instead of standing on the new and safe ground, an immense effort would be expended in a fruitless attempt to stay with the lost reality.

Help could be found in the support of those who have already reached a certain level of attunement to the new spatial conditions. Yet the dream issues a warning. Instead of being open to the offered helping hand, the dreamer expresses doubt that standing in the new space is a safe alternative. Embodied human beings are so deeply attached to "normal" gravitational circumstances that their ability to react positively to the possible reset, or even to accept another's help, will be close to zero. How else to understand why the dreamer refuses help in making the last few steps that separate him from the safe place. The warning is to prepare now for a possible future inversion of our global space so as not to be caught by surprise.

The small dead bush in the dream represents the fabric of life. When complemented by the connection to the dragon powers, it represents the unshakable foundation of Gaia's universe – the foundation that can not be endangered. To this end, I can offer the following exercise:

- Be present and in peace. Sit down and choose a small plant to hold with your imagination in your lap.
- Fold your hands in the form of a cup to hold the chosen plant. Include in your imagination its roots, together with a clump of fertile earth.
- Then be aware that behind your back, at the level of the hips, there is a horizontal flow of Gaia's dragon power heading toward you simultaneously from the left and right. It feels like a thin but powerful beam of lava.
- The goal of the exercise is to merge the subtle and wet quality of the plant with the strong and fiery presence of the primeval power of Gaia – without burning the elemental essence of the plant.
- The merging takes place at the center of your belly space, the focus of your perfect presence while embodied within the manifested world.
- Hold the merged quality as long as needed, or as long as it gives you a valuable experience.

The exercise should be supported by following breathing pattern:

- Inhale the quality of the plant, leading the breath to the center of the belly. Exhale to fill the pelvic cavity with the plant essence.
- Then inhale from the dragon power behind your back and exhale into the space of the pelvic cavity.
- Repeat the breathing a few times, and then observe how the synthesis of both qualities comes into being. Distribute its quality around your body as a nourishing and protective sphere.

10
Earth Changes, human destiny, a path for hope!

The old world structure is falling apart, threatening to pull the life systems of the Earth into a whirlpool of destruction. As this book shows, it may not be a simple matter to orientate yourself among the manifold facets of the Earth transmuting process.

With the ongoing process of the changing Earth there are two main streams, running parallel to each other, that are trying to prepare for the coming changes, some parts intertwining so closely that it is not possible to separate them. On the one hand, wealthy nations are making extravagant, almost fantastical plans to protect their cities from the coming floods and earthquakes. On the other hand, there are individuals and groups that are developing alternative paths to reconnect with the Earth and nature, with the aim of supporting the creation of a new Earth body that would open new and healthy prospects for the future development of life and culture on our planet.

The following dream shows the deeper insight that the two currents cannot be separated and, even more, that the role of human beings can be to embody a creative connection between them:

I am observing the flight of two gigantic birds. They are strong and beautiful. They fly with the speed of light. The left one is a grey color and the right one is pure white. They seem to compete with each other. Which one will be the first to reach the distant goal? I notice that the white bird has a little bit of an advantage over the grey one.

The grey bird speaks to the white one in a language that I can understand: "I thought our goal is to be one and the same."
The statement is accompanied with the image of a baroque palace. The white bird answers with an image of an wide open shining landscape bursting with life.

I realize that speaking to the white bird was a trick from the grey bird. The enormous concentration of the white bird has been weakened for a moment, and the grey bird wins some advantage.

I am upset since I feel a sense of identity with the white bird. I know that becoming as one with the white bird can support it in this dramatic moment.

So, I try to stretch my leg out to push against the green slope beneath me as they are flying by. I know intuitively that pushing against the slope will help the white bird to regain its lost advantage.

But beware! In front is a high, steep concrete wall that will not allow me to push off from the living ground. I look at the green slope, knowing it to be the last chance for a rescuing push.

(This is only the first part of the dream – the second part, giving instructions on how to behave at this moment, comes later.)

The first part conveys the actual situation upon the deeper causal levels of the ongoing Earth Changes. There are two different possibilities on how the cluster of the earthly worlds could be developed. The urgency that accompanies the dream makes it clear that we have arrived at the moment to decide which path to take for the future.

In giving the image of a palace as its goal, the grey bird reveals itself as standing for a hierarchical order that shows no interest for the flow of life. Instead it is turned inward, into its closed structures. The vision of the grey bird can be identified with the high-tech society, which has lost interest in living nature, having as its goal to artificially produce everything that human culture needs to survive.

Contrary to the patriarchal order of the baroque palace, the white bird presents its goal with an image of openness, closeness to nature, and the freedom of being and creating. Supposing that the dreamer represents humanity. Thinking beyond the pressures of the ruling social, political and economic patterns, it feels absolutely normal that he identifies himself with the vision of the white bird. Deeply within, he knows that at this moment the priority for our generation's incarnation upon the Earth is to contribute whatever it needs so that the evolution of the earthly universe can follow the vision of the white bird.

What should not be overlooked is the urgency inherent in the dream. It says that without the cooperation of human beings, Gaia cannot open the new path of freedom and cooperation among all living beings. Human beings have the ability to consciously co-facilitate the quantum leap that can open the path that is in tune with the new constitution of the universe. But what can be done practically at this moment of decision?

Luckily, the dreamer remembers the second part of the dream, which has practical instructions. It consist of three sequences.

Dream Sequence 1

I am part of a group of people dedicated to some selfless activity. The telephone rings with an invitation from Brazil that our group should take part in an intercontinental meditation to be started in a few minutes. I am excited to make the invitation known to the group. Just in that moment, everybody from the group declares that they have have an urgent task to do. One by one, the members leave, and I am alone.

The first point shows how important it is to connect with and work in groups and networks. The single human being cannot enact the needed contribution to the Earth's quantum leap that is required to reach the new level of evolution. The attuned presence of a number of different groups and communities is required in the process. Unfortunately, human culture often misinterprets the principle of "free will" as permission to make arbitrary decisions and take egocentric action, instead of understanding it as an invitation to create freely for the good of the whole and for all other beings.

Dream Sequence 2

I am convinced that it is absolutely necessary to build railway tracks up to the peak of a mountain. A great effort will be needed to bring up a steam locomotive. Finally the difficult transport succeeds. Only then, I become aware of how crazy and senseless this action is. I am now deeply worried on how to bring the locomotive down again. I find inner peace through the Greek philosopher Heraclitus, who said: "The way up and the way down are one and the same."

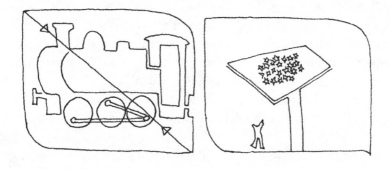

The second instruction, based upon the saying of Heraclitus, illuminates the waste of energy in worrying about the processes of decay that are observed and experienced within modern society, politics, and the economy. The difficult transportation of an old-fashioned locomotive up the hill is a symbol of a modern civilization that has lost connection with the functioning of living organisms. Instead of letting yourself to be caught up in the rescue of the Earth's current atmosphere and biotopes, you should engage in creating new conditions for life and its beings, humanity included. Do not worry. In the meantime, there will be as well active groups and individuals who will understand the call of Gaia in such a way as to engage with her in protecting nature and the conditions for life upon the planet.

Dream Sequence 3

I am observing a high-placed steel platform. At first I am convinced that the platform was built for the locomotive in the previous dream sequence to be exhibited as a monument honoring the achievements of human civilization. But now I realize that the platform's surface has been treated with a thin black film that would be destroyed by the heavy locomotive. I try to figure out why the purpose of the platform was changed. The clue is found in the shiny sparks distributed on the black film.

On awakening from the dream, I understand that the platform was being prepared for the needed push-off to accelerate the flight of the white bird, assuring that it not be overcome by the grey bird. This last sequence of the instructions informs me that it is not too late to act to benefit the white bird ... *the successful transition from the age of the Earth element to the one governed by the freedom of the Air element.* We are now in the midst of the preparations for decisive actions. Get ready!

This book, which we have walked through together, offers many possibilities of where to start and what to do – primarily inwardly, within oneself, but also in the light of the day.

Conclusion

How would the creation of a new Earth sphere affect the future of humanity?

I was extremely happy to have finished the present book after two month of work. I had already decided to throw my computer out the window and go to the Bahamas. But then a dear friend of mine pointed out that I had not shared my insights concerning the hottest question, "How is the creation of the new Earth sphere going to affect our everyday life?" So, I have brought the computer back into my office, replaced the broken parts, and written this conclusion.

To answer the question, it would be best to revisit a dream that I published sometime during the last few years. I've forgot where. Never mind. The dream goes like this:

We are traveling on an ordinary local train until it comes to a stop when the locomotive is so seriously broken that we are not sure if it will ever be possible to repair it. The place where we are in the train is a lonely place, and there is nowhere to go to drink coffee or play roulette. Bored travelers walk in and out of the train, speaking to each other through the open windows, etc.

Suddenly the news reaches us that an express train is approaching on the same track. We panic. We are sure that there will be a terrible crash!

A few moments later the express train arrives. There is no crash. It simply drives right through the old train. The new train is composed of light.

The language of the dream is excellent in painting the actual situation on the planet in a simple way. Autocratic regimes pop up to hold millions, even billions, of people chained to their ideological dogmas or to the egocentric ambitions of the leaders. The way of life based upon a linear economy and fossil fuels flourishes even though we all know that we are heading toward planetary suicide. New technologies appear daily, dragging masses of people into virtual spaces that have lost any connection to living nature. The broken train of human civilization stands blocked upon the track of its evolution.

The arriving light train represents the new space of reality being built by Gaia and her spiritual helpers to become embodied as a new kind of planetary space. It is obvious that the construction of a new Earth sphere is under way at many different levels, offering new solutions to the seemingly irresolvable problems of our age.

The dream uses the image of a light train because the new Earth sphere is composed of lighter and quicker vibrations than the Earth built upon the laws and qualities of the element Earth. We are entering the age of the much lighter and movable element Air (as explained in the first chapter of this book).

The dream is very clear that the express train does not simply over-run the old one. On the contrary, it even shows itself as being present for a certain span of time inside the old train. If we travelers would be attentive, we could just sit down in the seats of the express train and continue upon the track of our evolution in the "light train"! How easy a solution to the greatest problems of our time this would be!

Having the above dream in mind, I dare to say that we human beings presently exist inside the blessed moment when the light train is still present within the old world structure. There is still enough time to sit down into its comfortable seats and continue the journey. But be aware! Though cosmic moments indeed are much longer than ours, yet there will come the moment when the express train will pass us by. Do not hesitate! Use the opportunity of the moment and tune your presence to the Air element planet – there are a number of rituals and exercises offered in this book for this purpose.

Now let us imagine that the light train has passed on, and some of us were not attentive enough, standing outside the train, smoking our cigarettes and chatting. We have missed the light train. What are our possibilities for the future like? We will most certainly not be alone, but will share our destiny with millions of people who cling to the old. The following dream from November 2019 gives a possible answer to that question. The first part of my dream paints the chaotic situation characteristic of present-day humanity:

I wake up during the night in a hotel, needing to pee. I follow the corridor to a door with the label WC – Gents. I open the door, but inside is a private bedroom. An angry man leaps up in his bed. Since the need is great, I decide to go to the WC – Ladies. While I am there, a woman enters and directs angry words at me. Ashamed, I return to my room, counting the doors so as not to enter a wrong room again.

The second part of the dream pinpoints the danger that is posed if the living links between the two parties involved in the Earth Changes are broken. Consequently, humanity would be divided into two totally separate parts: those who are attached to the mass consciousness, in the following dream those who are traveling in the bus, and the alternative, those who are represented by the dreamer riding a bicycle:

I decide to travel throughout Italy on a tourist bus.
Unfortunately, all the seats are already reserved, so I must ride my bicycle behind the bus. The problem is that the bus is much quicker than the cyclist. Since dinner and the hotel rooms are to be shared, the question arises of where to meet each evening with the people on the bus. I propose going to a store and buying a map of Italy to clarify the places where the people from the bus and the cyclist would meet. But instead of a map, the salesperson offers a white sheet of paper where the distances between the various towns of Italy are written. I refuse this paper and ask the salesperson to look for a proper map. I am nervous because the bus will be leaving in four minutes.

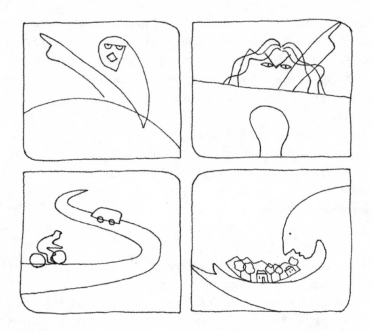

What the dreamer refuses is the concept of the separation of two world spheres with no living connection between them. The concept is symbolized by the list of the mere geographic distances between separate places. The dreamer's strong desire for a proper geographic map points toward a solution, grounded in such a way that humankind can still experience itself as one whole, even if this whole is composed of several relatively autonomous units.

There are several possible solutions. I am sure Gaia does not intend to abandon any of the human race, to leave anyone in darkness. On our way together through the landscape of this book, we emphasized that the influence of the element Air would push the manifested Earth to evolve further toward becoming a multidimensional planet. As a result, there is the possibility that the various groups of human souls could find, within one and the same planetary space, the conditions that each of them needed for their further development. The diversity that would come into being would not separate but rather confirm the integrity of humanity and of our planet Earth.

Such a manifold planetary sphere will be the home of several parallel realities offered to human souls when they prepare to embody upon the Earth. Souls that need to work on the individual burdens that prevented them from joining the "light express" will be drawn to the dimension of the Earth where they will find optimal conditions to detach from alienated patterns, to transmute their traumas, and become beings of freedom and peace. In this dimension, Gaia's elemental intelligence will be the teacher, inspiring people while they face the difficult processes of transmutation. But the main teacher will be the complicated transformation process itself, through which the more and more deserted present planet will become again a planet of nature's pristine beauty and strength.

Those souls who have already gone through the transformation process may incarnate there to help the souls who have stayed behind during the birth of the Air-element Earth. I believe also that other beings, especially the elemental beings of the Fifth element, will be ready to support the transmuting processes of those who in the dream travel in the "bus" of the mass consciousness. Gaia has taught these elementals how to understand human beings and how to cooperate with them.

For the other souls – represented by the bicyclist in the dream – who are ready for the subtle conditions of the Air-element Earth, possibilities will be offered to work on developing Earth's multidimensional space while collaborating with the parallel evolutions. The expression "to work on" is not actually adequate because in the conditions of the new space "working" is identical with "being." The world sphere of the Air element is so subtle that it can exist only if it can lean upon the love and consciousness dimension of those beings that constitute its globe. This means that communication and creative imagination are equal to existence. The souls that decide to manifest in the condition of the new Earth will have to learn how to be creative in the new conditions – not just as individuals but, more important, in groups – cooperating with all the other spheres of the Earth's cluster and its beings.

Another, equally important option is that some souls may decide to cooperate with Gaia and her elemental helpers in transforming the rather deserted Earth of the element Earth back to its original beauty and primordial strength. Through cooperative creative efforts, the "old" Earth will become part of the new Earth's cluster, as one of its dimensions. I can see it as a kind of planetary park where nature will be offering the possibilities to create one's own paradise, vibrating as an autonomous dimension but being at the same time part of the undivided multidimensional planet. Beings from other spheres of the Earth – human beings and beings from other evolutions – will be invited to visit and enjoy the kingdom of nature, its peace and wisdom.

APPENDIX

1 A multidimensional model of reality

On reading this book, it becomes obvious that I use a specific model of spatial dimensions to be able to recognize the existence of those beings and phenomena that are not of the material Earth and yet are an inevitable part of the life processes upon the Earth. I wish to outline this specific model, to be used by the reader as a key to finding a better approach to the themes discussed in the book.

The model of the multidimensional reality that I use was developed during thirty years of work with the Earth healing processes in many cities and landscapes worldwide. This kind of work partly evolved in groups, through cooperation with interested people, and partly through lithopuncture – positioning stones with carved cosmograms on specific places.

Basically the model comprises three levels, each consisting of three dimensions:

– Earthly causal realms, representing the planetary matrix of life (D 1-3)
– Embodied reality, or the manifested world (D 4-6)
– Cosmic causal realms, representing the universal matrix of creation (D 7-9)

The embodied reality is that realm where the creative impulses from the core of Gaia and the ones from the widths of the universe meet to interact and create the marvel of the embodied world. But it is not just materialized reality (D 5) that constitutes the manifested world. It is supported by the capacity of the planetary watery sphere (D 6), which holds coded all the information needed for the creative consciousness of the elemental beings (D 4) to mold the etheric forms of planetary phenomena. In the fifth dimension, elemental beings are partly manifest in materialized form and partly in subtle (energy-like) form.

The manifested world is rooted in the worlds of both the earthly causal and cosmic causal (D 1-3 and D 7-9). These are presented in depth throughout the book and also in this drawing.

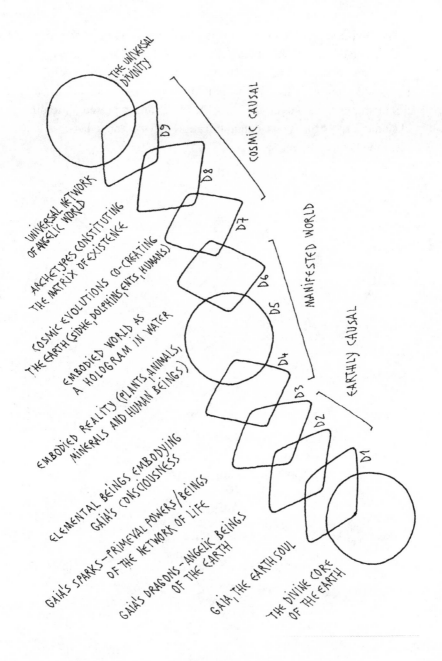

THE UNIVERSAL DIVINITY

D9

COSMIC CAUSAL

D8

UNIVERSAL NETWORK OF ANGELIC WORLD

ARCHETYPES CONSTITUTING THE MATRIX OF EXISTENCE

D7

COSMIC EVOLUTIONS CO-CREATING THE EARTH (SIDHE, DOLPHINS, ENTS, HUMANS)

D6

MANIFESTED WORLD

D5

EMBODIED WORLD AS A HOLOGRAM IN WATER

EMBODIED REALITY (PLANTS, ANIMALS, MINERALS AND HUMAN BEINGS)

D4

EARTHLY CAUSAL

D3

ELEMENTAL BEINGS EMBODYING GAIA'S CONSCIOUSNESS

D2

GAIA'S SPARKS - PRIMEVAL POWERS/BEINGS OF THE NETWORK OF LIFE

D1

GAIA'S DRAGONS - ANGELIC BEINGS OF THE EARTH

GAIA, THE EARTH SOUL

THE DIVINE CORE OF THE EARTH

The Divinity, as the unifying principle, finds its home at the core of the universe (Sophia) as well as at the core of the Earth (Gaia).

Relating to the model, I wish to emphasize the importance of the intersection places, where each rhombus or circle – indicating the different dimensions – overlap. These intersections represent interdimensional portals that make communication and exchange between single dimensions possible.

2 How to use Gaia Touch exercises and rituals

In addition to the text and drawings, some exercises and Gaia Touch personal rituals are presented throughout the book.

This book is not intended to project my intellectual ideas upon the reader but to offer my personal experiences, insights, and dreams related to the process of the Earth Changes. With the same intent, I propose the Gaia Touch exercises and body rituals so that you can have your own experience of a given theme.

The exercises that I create are not visualizations, even if images are often used as the means to enter into the experience. Visualizations have a mental character and can not open a direct door to the experience. In our case, the exercises are based upon the creative capacity of imagination.

Imagination is the human capacity to create inner images linked with the so-called "power of the word." In this case, one does not create images from the mental level of one's consciousness but from the consciousness of the heart, rooted in the dragon powers of the pelvic cavity – the belly. Under such conditions, the proposed exercises open a direct path to the searched-for experience.

Gaia Touch hand and body rituals are presented throughout the book. Here I include some practical instructions on using the exercises:

- Choose two or three Gaia Touch body or hand rituals and perform them over a certain period of time, with the aim to experience changes within your inner world and the subtle body constitution.

- You can perform these exercises equally well in a 15th floor apartment as in a place in nature. The exercises do not demand a specific environment. They create their own subtle environment as you do them. (Exceptions are some of the walking exercises that need a natural ambience to be performed.)

- When you are doing the body exercises in the sitting position, make sure that your backbone is straight, in a natural manner.
- It does not matter what time of the day or within what conditions you work with Gaia Touch exercises.
- It can be an even more valuable experience when the exercises are performed in a group.
- The hand rituals can also be done while sitting but, again, make sure that your backbone is straight so that it can vibrate with the exercise.
- Some of the rituals may need to be done rhythmically; some work the best if performed very slowly. Your feeling will tell you which is the best way to perform them in the given moment.
- Gaia Touch is an open system, so feel free to discover your own rituals and exercises by developing them yourself through your intimate connection with Gaia's universe, her places, and beings.

If you would like to work more extensively with the Gaia Touch exercises and rituals, see *Universe of the Human Body,* published by Lindisfarne Books, available at www.steinerbooks.org and the *Gaia Touch Card Set* (published both in English and German), available at www.geniusloci-publishing.com

Cosmogram of Gaia Touch exercises and rituals

3 The feminine chakra system

Since the twenty-chakra feminine system can play an important role in balancing the overemphasized seven-chakra masculine culture of our present time, it could be helpful to present it more in detail as an inspiration to use it in your daily life.

The feminine chakra system has a circular form that connects us to the cyclical quality of the feminine principle. The heart chakra represents the center of four chakra circles. Each circle connects to one of the four elements of Gaia's creation. Through collaboration with the elements of Water, Fire, Earth and Air, the feminine principle gives birth to the manifested reality. (See the image of the five-element feminine chakra system, p. 87, which shows the twenty chakras of the feminine chakra system.)

The four chakras of the element Water (element Water represents the flow of life):

- The pair of chakras under the clavicles is responsible for informing the water sphere of the human being with all the codes and archetypes needed to create, in each moment, the human body as a micro-universe.

- The pair of chakras at the lower end of the thorax manages the flow of the Water element between the body and its natural or cosmic environment.

The circular movement of life energy between the four chakras of the Water element constitutes the human body as a watery sphere.

The six chakras of the element Fire (element Fire represents the power that moves the life processes, the processes of transmutation):

- The two Fire element chakras positioned at the edge of the hips work to bring dynamic to the body's life processes at the organic level.

- The pair of chakras at the outer edge of the shoulder bones is responsible for the exchange of the sparks of life between the body and the environment.
- The pair of chakras at the ear lobes works to activate cosmic impulses, so that the personal life can become a pilgrimage upon the path of our spiritual evolution.

The five chakras of the element Earth (element Earth is responsible for the processes of embodiment):

- The pair of chakras behind the knees holds the human soul present within the condition of embodiment.
- The chakra between the knees is responsible for the grounding of the body.
- The pair of chakras behind the elbows makes possible the embodiment of creative ideas and plans.

To be able to perceive the positions of the chakras corresponding to the elements of Earth and Air, one should stand up with the arms outstretched.

The five chakras of the element Air (element Air represents the processes of communication):

- The pair of chakras on the soles of the feet is capable of holding active the vertical path of communication between Earth and Cosmos.
- The pair of chakras on the palms of the hands has the task of upholding the path of communication between the manifested and causal worlds.
- The chakra above the head is positioned as high as the human hand can reach. It makes possible the communication between the individual and the spiritual world of the ancestors and descendants.

The heart chakra represents the center and the Fifth element in the context of the feminine chakra system. It can be considered as the causal (archetypal) background of the four elements. It is also the point of connection between the feminine chakra system and the chakras of the masculine system, positioned vertically along the backbone and beyond. "Beyond" means that the masculine chakra system has new extensions to become a twelve-chakra ladder:

– Two additional chakras, one between the knees and one under the feet, connect the human being to Gaia's universe.
– Three additional chakras, above the crown chakra, connect the human being to various dimensions of Sophia's universe.
– Besides the heart chakra, there are two other chakras that connect the masculine with the feminine system, the one between the knees (element Earth chakra) and the highest one above the head (element Air chakra).

To activate the foot chakras one can use the walking exercises presented on pp. 82 ff. To relate to the chakras above the head look at the Gaia Touch exercise that connects to the dragon power within on pp. 23-24.

The following Gaia Touch exercise can help to strengthen the feminine chakra system:

Gaia Touch exercise to get in touch with the five elements within our body

- Start by tapping three times on the center of your chest to mark the presence of the heart system, representing the integrating Fifth element. All five fingers are united into a fist while tapping upon the chest.
- Continue with the activation of the Water element by rubbing for a while, with the hands crossed, the two points on the chest below the clavicles, where the two chakras of the Water element are located.

- Now move to the element of Fire by rubbing the earlobes for a while, because two Fire-element chakras are situated there. The hands do not cross this time.
- Next is the element Earth. The corresponding chakras are located behind the knees. Tap, with the hands crossed, on your kneecaps.
- Finally we come to the element Air, with the chakras in the middle of the palms. To activate them, one should clap once with your hands in front of your body and once more behind the back.
- Start the sequence again by tapping upon the chest.

4 How to survive in the conditions of intense Earth Changes

The Earth is walking her path of changes with great speed while humanity, in general, has no idea what is going on, and consequently our collaboration with Gaia is weak and slow. This contradictory situation may cause humanity to find itself temporarily in a space deprived of needed life-forces and creative inspirations. To get ready for such a possible situation we should start practicing now.

The following two meditations can help to open the channels needed to receive and integrate the primeval powers of the Earth and universe into our body and environment. These channels can serve the elemental beings to "feed" all of us with the life energy and the spatial conditions we need to continue living our life in a creative way, collaborating with Gaia's intent to create an age of peace and integrity for all upon our planet.

Meditation 1

Start by opening to the primeval powers of Gaia. Imagine that a double vortex is spinning around your coccyx.

The two components of the vortex go slowly apart and come together again. Repeat this opening of the door a few times. Between the opening and closing make a short pause.

During one of these pauses inhale the primeval (dragon) power and consciousness from the core of the Earth. Lead it up to the center of the elemental heart, which pulsates under the point of the lowest breastbone.

Exhale it from that same point so that the breath, loaded with the primeval powers of the Earth, passes the sphere of your body and continues into your environment.

Repeat this exercise a few times.

Meditation 2

Open the highest point of your skull. Imagine that the bones composing the skull slide apart in the way that the continental plates do at times. The opening that comes into being is what naturally occurs in newborn babies, the fontanel.

Slide the bones apart slowly and then close the opening again. Do this a few times. Between the opening and closing make a short pause.

During one of these pauses inhale the primeval (spiritual) power and consciousness from the core of the universe. Lead it down to the heart center.

From there, exhale it so that the breath, loaded with the primeval powers of the universe, passes the sphere of your body and continues into your environment.

Repeat this exercise a few times.

Give thanks.

List of Gaia Touch Exercises and Rituals

Gaia Touch hand exercise to tune to the new epoch of the Air element   13

Gaia Touch hand exercise to promote the creation of the new space   16

Gaia Touch exercise to connect with the inner dragon power   23

Gaia Touch exercise to transmute the dragon slayer pattern   25

Gaia Touch ritual to open your multidimensional body   41

Personal ritual of the Healing Tear of Grace   48

Gaia Touch hand ritual of detachment (No. 1, Bali version)   50

Gaia Touch personal ritual to connect with your inner animal   57

Gaia Touch ritual to connect with the three aspects of the elemental self   64

Gaia Touch ritual to delete outdated links and create new links   74

Gaia Touch body ritual to open your heart system – short version   77

Gaia Touch body ritual to open your heart system – longer version   79

Gaia Touch exercise to open your heart system – complete version   80

Gaia Touch personal ritual to connect with the world of the dolphins   101

Gaia Touch body ritual to connect with the world of the Sidhe   104

Exercise (proposed by an Ent) to connect with the world of the Ents   108

Gaia Touch hand ritual to experience the plant core of the human body   113

Gaia Touch personal ritual to connect with the creative network of Indigo Gaia   129

Gaia Touch hand ritual of detachment – (No. 2 version)   136

Gaia Touch hand ritual of protection with the help of the mandorla form   137

Marko Pogačnik (b. 1944) lives with his wife and collaborator Marika in Šempas, Slovenia. In the 1960s he worked as a conceptual and land-artist as a member of the OHO group, a Slovene artist collective and a significant movement in the context of Slovene national culture, Yugoslavian socialistic culture and international youth culture. It was the first 'radical urban-ideological' artistic appearance in Slovene modern arts. Marko later developed Lithopuncture, a method of Earth healing using cosmograms carved on stone pillars. For 22 years he has focused on collaborating with the Earth-changing process. In this context, he developed Gaia Touch body exercises and the vision of a Geoculture. Since 2005 he has built Geopuncture stone circles worldwide, together with an international team of colleagues. In 2016 he was appointed as Artist for Peace and UNO Goodwill Ambassador by the Secretary General of UNESCO. His books in English include, among others: *Elemental Beings and Nature Spirits*, *Turned Upside Down*, *Sacred Geography*, *Gaia's Quantum Leap*, *Universe of the Human body*, and *Christ Power and Earth Wisdom*.

www.markopogacnik.com

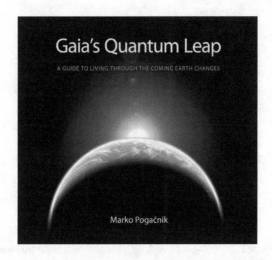

Gaia's Quantum Leap

A GUIDE TO LIVING THROUGH THE COMING EARTH CHANGES

Marko Pogačnik

With his deep psychic sensitivity and extensive experience in exploring the landscape experientially through geomancy, Marko Pogačnik helps us understand and attune to the epochal Earth changing process that is dancing in and around us.

Recalling 63 dramatic dreams as stories illustrated with original drawings, he crafts a way for us through these deep changes, bringing remedies, insights, and exercises that will help us to adapt and survive, and help Gaia bring forth her true self.

GAIA'S QUANTUM LEAP
A Guide to Living through the Coming Earth Changes
Lindisfarne Books / 978-1-58420-089-5

MARKO POGAČNIK

Sacred Geography

GEOMANCY: CO-CREATING THE EARTH COSMOS

Geomancy is an ancient word that derives from the Greek word "Gaia" meaning Earth Goddess and "Manteia" meaning study or divination. Marko Pogačnik calls geomancy "sacred geography," a spiritual study of place and landscape.

This book is a guide to the hidden dimensions of over 170 locations around the world. Illustrated with original drawings by the author, it presents a holistic approach to the Earth as a conscious creative being.

Besides comprehensive information about geomantic phenomena and elemental beings, Marko gives practical methods on how to widened our perception and develop our own experiences while exploring places and landscapes.

SACRED GEOGRAPHY
Geomancy: Co-Creating the Earth Cosmos
Lindisfarne Books / 978-1-58420-054-3

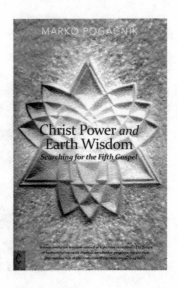

Based on methods of investigation and perception that he has developed over many decades of work in healing the Earth's landscapes, in communication with his elemental master and with the spiritual world, Marko Pogačnik discovers that woven invisibly into the four canonical Gospels is Christ's message concerning how to live positively at the threshold of the third millennium — a Fifth Gospel. Bringing together knowledge of the elemental beings, Earth science, and Christ, the hidden message of Christ's words are uncovered.

This 2020 edition of the Findhorn Press edition from 1999 is enriched with new information and offers an important update on methods you can use to gain a broader, spiritual perception of today's reality.

CHRIST POWER AND EARTH WISDOM
Searching for the Fifth Gospel
Clairview Books / 978-1-91299-210-2

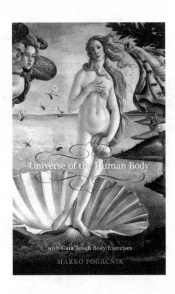

Using his experience exploring the landscape through geomantic work, Marko Pogačnik approaches the human body with a similar kind of multidimensional perception. In this unique book, he explores how we can consciously enter our own body space to experience it from the inside and activate our potentials in order to prepare our body for the challenges of the Earth Changes.

This book is both theoretical and practical. It includes exercises called Gaia Touch exercises, a combination of imaginations and body movements in the form of body "cosmograms," that can be perceived and understood by other beings of the Earth and the cosmos. These exercises stimulate personal development and help us become conscious co-creators with Gaia of the new emerging reality.

UNIVERSE OF THE HUMAN BODY
With Gaia Touch Body Exercises
Lindisfarne Books / 978-1-58420-986-7